Good Essay Writing

A Social Sciences Guide

Good Essay Writing

A Social Sciences Guide

Second Edition

Peter Redman

The Open University

in association with

 SAGE Publications

London • Thousand Oaks • New Delhi

ISBN 0-7619-7204-8 (hbk)
ISBN 0-7619-7205-6 (pbk)
© The Open University 2001
First published 2001
Reprinted 2003, 2004

This publication is strongly recommended for Open University courses.
Details of Open University courses can be obtained from the Call Centre,
PO Box 724, The Open University, Milton Keynes MK7 6ZS,
United Kingdom: tel. +44 (0)1908 653231, e-mail ces-gen@open.ac.uk
Alternatively, you may visit the Open University website at
http:www.open.ac.uk where you can learn more about the wide range of
courses and packs offered at all levels by The Open University.
For availability of other course components, contact Open University
Worldwide Ltd, The Berrill Building, Walton Hill, Milton Keynes MK7
6AA, United Kingdom tel: +44 (0)-1908-858785; fax +44 (0)-1908-858787;
e-mail ouwenq©open.ac.uk; website http://www.ouw.co.uk

SAGE Publications Ltd
1 Oliver's Yard, 55 City Road
London EC1Y 1SP

SAGE Publications Inc
2455 Teller Road
Thousand Oaks, California 91320

SAGE Publications India Pvt Ltd
B–42 Panchsheel Enclave
PO Box 4109
New Delhi 110 017

British Library Cataloguing in Publication data
A catalogue record for this book is available from the British Library

Typeset by Mayhew Typesetting, Rhayader, Powys
Printed and bound in Great Britain by
Biddles Ltd, King's Lynn, Norfolk

CONTENTS

....

PREFACE TO THE SECOND EDITION

....

Good Essay Writing was originally written for the use of Open University students studying the social sciences at undergraduate level. Its success with OU students led us to think that *Good Essay Writing* may be of value to a wider undergraduate audience. As a result, we have taken the opportunity to revise and update the guide, partly for the continuing benefit of OU students, but also with the needs of this wider social science audience in mind.

There is, of course, an existing range of material offering excellent advice and guidance on undergraduate essay writing. Indeed, some of these publications are suggested as further reading in Appendix F of this guide. *Good Essay Writing* aims to complement rather than supplant these resources. In particular, it is not intended as an intensive, interactive course in essay writing. For this, students will need to look elsewhere. Instead, *Good Essay Writing* offers a practical, quick reference guide to essay writing skills and conventions in the social sciences in a form that is, we believe, brief, affordable and easily accessible.

Books are never written by a single author and this is particularly true of *Good Essay Writing*, which not only draws on existing OU materials and good practice but has been prepared for the Social Sciences Faculty as a result of a collective effort. The first edition was initiated in the Open University in the East Midlands by a team of Associate Lecturers, and was the brain-child of Helen Lentell, then Staff Tutor in the Social Sciences Faculty. Peter Redman was the main author of the first edition, while Helen Lentell, Sue Cole, Rosie Collins, Rick Davies, Peter Hull, Mary Larkin, Liz Ockleford, Isobel Shelton and Andy Sutton all contributed to early drafts. Our thanks to them. Chris Brook, Ross Fergusson, Chris Nichols, Diane Watson and Helen Westcott provided later additional material, and Jonathan Davies designed the book. Peggotty Graham co-ordinated the project and contributed to the content of the final version. Our thanks to them all.

This new edition was revised and updated by Peter Redman with kind advice and assistance from Geraldine Carpenter, Vicki Goodwin, Mary Langan, Janet Macdonald, Alison Rolfe and Lynne Slocombe. It was edited by Lynne Slocombe.

We hope that you find *Good Essay Writing* useful and enjoyable.

Good luck with your studies!

Peter Redman,
on behalf of the project team.

1 INTRODUCTION

....

- How to use this guide
- Will the guide tell me everything about essay writing?
- Where to go for further help

....

Many students, however experienced, find essay writing difficult. Many, particularly those returning to study after a long break, find essay writing daunting. There is, of course, no guaranteed recipe for a good essay, no absolute method. However, it is the purpose of this book to recommend and illustrate proven approaches and techniques which, combined with practice, will increase your confidence and skill and thereby improve the quality and effectiveness of your writing.

Throughout the book you will find examples of good practice in essay writing that will help you in this task. These include how to: 'wordstorm' your initial ideas, organize and plan your essay, write effective introductions and conclusions, build an effective argument, use evidence, and provide accurate references. Summary sections help to reinforce your understanding of these issues, while extracts from academic texts and sample essays – including examples of good and poor answers – help illustrate the points being made. These all serve to demonstrate how a very rough jumble of words really can be transformed into the clear flowing prose of a well written essay.

Good Essay Writing is partly intended for Open University (OU) students working on courses in the social sciences. As a result, you will find that some of the content is highlighted for the particular attention of OU students.

This material usually refers to practices and procedures specific to the OU. You will also find that the OU term 'tutor' is used throughout as a generic description of a university teacher. However, the majority of the book is designed to be of benefit to any undergraduate student of the social sciences, whether studying with the OU or with another institution. If your aim is to write better essays and you want quick, practical advice and guidance that builds on years of successful and high quality teaching from the Open University, then *Good Essay Writing* is for you.

In brief, the guide aims:

- to introduce key essay writing skills and conventions to people who have not studied courses in the social sciences before;
- to recap on basic essay writing skills for those who have already done some studies in the social sciences or related areas;
- to introduce more advanced essay writing skills.

1.1 How to use this guide

Inevitably, some readers will be familiar with much of the material in *Good Essay Writing*. However, some aspects may be new to you, and other parts will help you build on or develop what you already know. As such, you should view *Good Essay Writing* as a resource that you can adapt to your own needs.

The sections that follow cover the main aspects of essay writing, ending with some general points to look out for.

Sections 2–6: provide a detailed outline of the qualities that are likely to characterize a social science essay in each of the different undergraduate grade bands and at different levels of writing experience; explore some basic principles of essay writing; provide recommendations on how to approach different types of essay questions; and discuss planning, preparation and writing introductions.

Section 7 looks at writing the main section of a social science essay, exploring how to structure an argument, how to support your case with evidence, and how to communicate your argument effectively.

Sections 8 and *9* discuss conclusion writing and explain how to compile references.

Section 10 looks at some common worries that people have about writing essays.

Section 11 consists of two examples of student essays – one strong, one weak.

After a few concluding remarks in *Section 12*, there are several appendices which contain important information on learning from past essays, 'process and command' words, using 'mind maps', referencing various sources, and academic abbreviations and 'foreign' words.

How can you use the guide most effectively? There are several approaches (as you can see from the bullet points below), and it will probably be best if you try to combine them to produce a strategy that works for you. Generally speaking, you can:

- read *Good Essay Writing* from cover to cover;
- skim read sections that you already know enough about;
- work systematically through sections such as 'Writing the main section';
- concentrate on the summaries at the end of each main section;
- use the contents pages and index to pinpoint particular issues that are relevant to you and ignore the rest;
- return to *Good Essay Writing* whenever you need to look up something or remind yourself of a particular point;
- use some sections as reference material, for example, some of the appendices.

1.2 Will the guide tell me everything about essay writing?

Good Essay Writing is a quick reference guide designed to help you build on your essay writing skills and to improve your abilities as a social scientist. It is not intended to –

nor could it – provide all the detailed guidance that you may need for each and every course that you study, nor does it cover more specialized tasks, such as project writing, how to handle graphs and tables and so on. Similarly, it is not intended as an extended, interactive course in essay writing. Its intention is to be short, practical and easily accessible.

As a result, we cannot promise to transform your essay writing overnight. The truth is that there is no magic formula that will guarantee you a good grade for every essay that you produce. In fact, there is no one 'correct' way to write an essay. Sometimes, the most exciting essays will be those that address a question in an unexpected way, that challenge its fundamental premises, or that succeed in producing new insights rather than recycling well-worn ideas. The advice in this guide suggests some generally agreed conventions, but these are not the only ones available and they do not by themselves add up to a great essay. Your essay writing will improve mainly through your own hard work in thinking things out for yourself, through experience, and through your increasing knowledge of the fields in which you work. 'How to . . .' guides like this one are rather like cookery books: they can tell you what the ingredients are, and they can suggest ways to mix the ingredients together. What they cannot do is turn you into a gourmet chef. Like cooking, essay writing is not something you ever stop learning about. However, we believe the advice in *Good Essay Writing* will help you to become more confident and more creative in your work.

1.3   Where to go for further help

Appendix F, 'Further reading', contains a range of material that you may find useful in developing your essay writing skills. Some of this material is interactive and offers more detailed advice and guidance than it is possible to include in a volume of this size; some provides more technical advice on specific aspects of writing.

Advice for OU students

If you want further help with essay writing, your tutor is the best person to advise you in the first instance. She or he may also be able to arrange extra support for you (either a 'special session' or 'telephone tutorial') or put you in touch with support that may be available from your Regional Centre. Your Regional Centre will also be able to supply you with the following Student Toolkits free of charge: *Effective Use of English* (Toolkit 1) and *Essay and Report Writing* (Toolkit 5). The 'Learner's Guide' website 'learning skills development' has further advice on writing skills (go to http://www.open.ac.uk/learners-guide). You should also check your course materials for advice specifically related to the needs of the course.

Finally, you should think about talking to fellow students. Many people will be having the same experiences as you, and you may well find that you learn more from sharing these experiences and looking through each other's essays than from any other source. Choose people with whom you feel comfortable working, discuss forthcoming essays together and swap assignments when they have been marked.

2 WHAT TUTORS LOOK FOR WHEN MARKING ESSAYS

....

- Marking schemes: criteria related to grade bands
- Writing skills: 'introductory', 'intermediate' and 'advanced' essays

....

One of the most frequent and reasonable questions that students ask is: What should I be doing to get a better grade? Of course, the answer to this question will depend on a number of factors. For example, what is required of an essay answer will clearly vary according to the precise question set. Equally, the standard expected of essay writing is likely to be higher on more advanced undergraduate courses than on those at entry level. Similarly, there may be higher expectations towards the end of a course than there were at its start. Having said this, it is possible to specify the various qualities (if only in general terms) that distinguish essays in the different grade bands, and what writing skills may be expected from essays at different levels.

Health warning

We have included this section to give you a *broad indication of what may be expected, in general, for different grades*. Increasingly, grade bands are defined in relation to 'learning outcomes' that draw on specified 'subject benchmarks' and 'key skills' (see, for example: http://www.qaa.ac.uk and http://www.qca.org.uk). Individual courses will have their own course-specific requirements for each of the grade ranges, and also the requirements will vary depending on whether the course is at a more or less advanced stage of undergraduate study. As a result, where they are available, you may want to look at the learning outcomes specified for your particular course of study. However, you should remember that grading an essay is always a matter of weighing up not only the structure, content and style of the essay, but the interplay between these, together with the interplay between any number of the different intellectual challenges built into the assignment. For all these reasons you should not expect the criteria for the gradings for a specific course to map exactly on to what we have set out here.

2.1 Marking schemes: criteria related to grade bands

In this section you will find guidelines adapted from those produced by the British Psychological Society (BPS, 1994) in conjunction with the Association of Heads of Psychology Departments. They do not correspond to the specific policy of the Open University or any other UK higher education institution, but they should give you an idea of the sorts of *general* things markers are likely to consider for different grade ranges. Remember, what is expected for a particular course for a particular grade may differ from these guidelines. Remember, too, you won't have to do well in every area to get a particular grade. For example, your depth of insight into theoretical issues may compensate for slightly weaker coverage of the evidence, or your understanding of the material may compensate for weaknesses in the coherence of your argument. It may also be the case that some of these criteria will be more relevant to advanced courses of undergraduate study (see Section 2.2 below).

Many of the terms used below (for example, 'developing an argument') are explored in greater detail in this guide. If you are unsure of their meaning, you may want to look them up.

Advice for OU students

Always remember to read the student notes for the specific assignment you are attempting and/or ask your tutor for guidance if you are unclear about what is expected of you.

Remember, particularly if you are new to the OU, that the University's marking scheme goes up to 100 and may be different from ones you have been used to in the past.

The criteria following the table indicate 'excellent', 'good pass', 'clear pass', 'bare pass', 'bare fail' and 'clear fail' essays. These categories broadly correspond to the following grade bands.

| | | Grade bands | |
OU	Conventional university		Other
85–100	1st	70+	A
70–84	2:1	60–69	B
55–69	2:2	50–59	C
40–54	3rd	40–49	D
30–39		30–39	Fail
0–29		0–29	Fail

An *excellent pass* is likely to:

- provide a comprehensive and accurate response to the question, demonstrating a breadth and depth of reading and understanding of relevant arguments and issues;
- show a sophisticated ability to synthesize a wide range of material;

- show a sophisticated ability to outline, analyse and contrast complex competing positions and to evaluate their strengths and weaknesses effectively;
- demonstrate clarity of argument and expression;
- develop a sophisticated argument, demonstrating logical reasoning and the effective use of well selected examples and evidence;
- where appropriate, demonstrate an ability to apply ideas to new material or in a new context;
- demonstrate depth of insight into theoretical issues;
- demonstrate an ability to write from 'within' a perspective or theory, including the ability to utilize appropriate social scientific concepts and vocabulary; may show a more creative or original approach (within the constraints of academic rigour);
- use a standard referencing system accurately.

A *good pass* is likely to:

- provide a generally accurate and well-informed answer to the question;
- be reasonably comprehensive;
- draw on a range of sources;
- be well organized and structured;
- demonstrate an ability to develop a strong and logical line of argument, supported by appropriate examples and evidence;
- show an ability to synthesize a wide range of material;
- show an ability to outline, analyse and contrast more complex competing positions, and to evaluate their strengths and weaknesses effectively;
- demonstrate the ability to work with theoretical material effectively and some confidence in handling social scientific concepts and vocabulary;
- where appropriate, demonstrate an ability to apply ideas to new material or in a new context;
- show a good understanding of the material;

- be clearly presented;
- use a standard referencing system accurately.

A *clear pass* is likely to:

- give an adequate answer to the question, though one dependent on commentaries or a limited range of source material;
- be generally accurate, although with some omissions and minor errors;
- develop and communicate a basic logical argument with some use of appropriate supporting examples and evidence;
- demonstrate an ability to synthesize a range of material;
- demonstrate an ability to outline, analyse and contrast competing positions, and to begin to evaluate their strengths and weaknesses (although this may be derivative);
- demonstrate a basic ability to address theoretical material and to use appropriate social scientific concepts and vocabulary;
- be written in the author's own words;
- show an understanding of standard referencing conventions, although containing some errors and omissions.

A *bare pass* is likely to:

- demonstrate basic skills in the areas identified in the 'clear pass' band

but may also:

- answer the question tangentially;
- miss a key point;
- contain a number of inaccuracies or omissions;

- show only sparse coverage of relevant material;
- fail to support arguments with adequate evidence;
- be over-dependent on source material;
- contain only limited references.

A *bare fail* is likely to:

- fail to answer the question;
- contain very little appropriate material;
- show some evidence of relevant reading but provide only cursory coverage with numerous errors, omissions or irrelevances such that the writer's understanding of fundamental points is in question;
- be highly disorganized;
- contain much inappropriate material;
- lack any real argument or fail to support an argument with evidence;
- demonstrate a lack of understanding of social scientific concepts and vocabulary and an inability to deploy social scientific writing skills such as skills of critical evaluation, synthesis, and so on;
- be unacceptably dependent on sources;
- be plagiarized (sometimes);
- demonstrate problems in the use of appropriate writing conventions such that the essay's meaning is systematically obscured.

A *clear fail* is likely to:

- show a profound misunderstanding of basic material;
- show a complete failure to understand or answer the question;
- provide totally inadequate information;
- be incoherent;
- be plagiarized (sometimes).

Essays are assessed not weighed

2.2   Writing skills: 'introductory', 'intermediate' and 'advanced' essays

As you move from entry level to more advanced under-graduate courses it is likely that you will be expected to develop and demonstrate an increasing range of essay writing skills. For example, you may be expected to write from 'within' a particular perspective, handle more complex theories or systematically interrogate original sources.

A general guide of this kind cannot give you a full breakdown of the skills that will be relevant to every course that you may take. What it tries to do is provide an outline of 'core' skills. Individual courses may emphasize different parts of these core skills or may involve specific skills of their own (for example, project writing, employing specific research methods, using graphs to present information). Individual essays may also require you to emphasize some 'core' skills more than others. As a result of these factors, you will need to adapt what we have set out below according to the demands of different questions and different courses.

We look now in detail at the various criteria that may be expected to distinguish a 'basic' or 'introductory' undergraduate essay from 'intermediate' and 'advanced' essays. Once again, many of these points are developed in later sections, so if you are not sure what the points mean (e.g. 'signposting', writing from 'within' a perspective), you may want to look them up.

Advice for OU students

The following criteria broadly map onto the OU's under-graduate courses in the social sciences at Levels 1, 2 and 3. Thus, having completed your Level 1 course you could be expected to have developed the various essay writing skills identified as appropriate to an 'introductory' essay. Remember, you would *not* necessarily be expected to have these skills already in place on starting an OU Level 1 course in the social sciences. Having developed these skills in the course of your Level 1 studies, you should be ready to tackle essay writing on a Level 2 course, where you would learn the skills identified as appropriate to an 'intermediate' essay.

The 'introductory' essay

Introductions are likely to demonstrate:

- a clear understanding of the scope of the question and what is required;
- the ability to 'signpost' the shape of the essay's argument clearly and concisely;
- a basic ability to define key terms.

Main sections are likely to demonstrate some or all of the following, depending on what the question requires:

- an ability to construct a basic argument that engages with the question;
- the ability to précis aspects of relevant material clearly and concisely, often relying on commentaries and other secondary sources;
- the ability to outline the basics of relevant theories;
- the ability to support arguments with appropriate evidence and examples drawn from different sources;
- an understanding that different theories are in competition, the ability to outline the main similarities and differences between these, and a basic ability to evaluate their strengths and weaknesses;
- an ability to utilize basic maps, diagrams and numerical data in a way that supports the discussion;
- some familiarity with major perspectives in the social sciences;
- some familiarity with relevant social scientific vocabulary.

Conclusions are likely to demonstrate:

- the ability to summarize the content of the essay clearly and concisely and to come to a conclusion.

Quotations should be referenced, and 'pass' essays will always need to avoid plagiarism. Essays should 'flow' smoothly, use sentences, paragraphs and grammar correctly, and be written in clear English.

The 'intermediate' essay

In addition to skills in all the above areas, intermediate essays may also show the following.

Introductions are likely to demonstrate:

- a clear understanding of more complex essay questions;
- a basic ability to 'signpost' the content as well as the shape or structure of the essay but not in a laboured way;
- a grasp of the major debates that lie 'behind the question';
- an ability to define key terms.

Main sections are likely to demonstrate some or all of the following, depending on what the question requires:

- the ability to construct more complex arguments relevant to the question;
- the ability to 'weight' different aspects of the material according to their significance within the overall argument;
- an ability to identify and précis the key debates relevant to the question;
- the ability to outline more complex theories in a basic form;
- an ability to relate abstract ideas and theories to concrete detail;
- an ability to support arguments with appropriate evidence and examples;
- an ability to utilize information drawn from across a wide range of source materials;
- the ability to make more complex evaluations of the strengths and weaknesses of competing positions and make a reasoned choice between these;
- an ability to utilize more complex maps, diagrams and numerical data;
- a preliminary ability to work from original texts and data without relying on commentaries on these;
- increased familiarity with major social scientific perspectives and social scientific vocabulary and increased confidence in applying these to specific issues;
- a preliminary ability to write from 'within' specific perspectives or theories;

- an ability to pull together different aspects of the course and to apply these to the essay;
- a basic ability in selecting and using appropriate quotations from, and making references to, key texts in the field.

Conclusions are likely to demonstrate:

- an ability to highlight the essay's core argument;
- the ability to provide a basic summary of the key debates raised by the question and the ability to provide an overview of 'current knowledge';
- a preliminary ability to point to absences in the argument or areas worthy of future development.

Essays should also be properly referenced, be written in the author's own words, and utilize a more developed and fluent writing style (for example, by handling transitions effectively).

The 'advanced' essay

In addition to skills in all of the above areas, advanced essays may also show the following.

Introductions are likely to demonstrate:

- the ability to present a more sophisticated version of the essay's core argument;
- the ability to summarize in more sophisticated forms the key debates raised by the question;
- the ability to provide more sophisticated definitions of terms;
- an ability to really interrogate the question by focusing on ideas or sub-questions prompted by the question in hand.

Main sections are likely to demonstrate some or all of the following:

- the ability to construct complex arguments, 'weighting' each section according to its significance within the overall argument;
- the ability to provide sophisticated outlines of complex theories;
- the ability to support arguments with appropriate evidence and examples drawn from a wide range of sources, and to use evidence *selectively* in a way that supports central points;
- the ability to evaluate competing positions and the confidence to write from 'within' a specific perspective or theory on the basis of a reasoned understanding of its strengths and weaknesses;
- familiarity with, and confidence in, handling complex maps, diagrams and numerical data;
- familiarity with, and confidence in, handling original texts and data without relying on commentaries;
- familiarity with the major social scientific perspectives and social scientific vocabulary, and confidence in applying these to specific issues and to new contexts;
- the ability to pull together different aspects of the course and apply these to the issues raised by a specific essay question;
- the ability to use appropriate quotations and cite key texts in the field.

Conclusions are likely to demonstrate:

- the ability to present a sophisticated summary of the essay's core argument;
- the ability to provide an effective synthesis of the key debates raised by the question, or a sophisticated overview of the state of 'current knowledge';
- a developed ability to point to absences in the argument or areas worthy of future development.

'Advanced' essays should be fully referenced and written in your own words. The best essays are likely to show a significant depth of understanding of the issues raised by the question and may show a more creative or original approach (within the constraints of academic rigour).

Different skills, same writer

In thinking about the requirements of different levels of essay writing, it is important to realize that different levels of skills do not come neatly packaged. For instance, you may already have advanced essay writing skills even while working at an introductory level of undergraduate study. Alternatively, you may have advanced skills of analysis (such as the ability to break down a complex argument into its component parts and summarize these effectively), but be struggling with the handling of theoretical concepts and perspectives. Or you may be very effective at your essay introductions, but more shaky when it comes to putting the argument together in the main section. The important point is that what we have set out are *indications* of what may be expected at different levels across the whole range of abilities, *not* that you must be able to demonstrate the appropriate level of ability in all cases. Remember, too, that an essay is always greater than its component parts, and it is how you put all those parts together that is often as important as the parts themselves.

....

Summary

- Essays are graded on extent to which they demonstrate of an understanding of relevant course content and of social scientific and writing skills.

- The exact mix of content and skills required will depend on the course and question. However, it is possible to specify in general terms what is expected for each grade band.

- As you become increasingly experienced, you should expect your understanding of social scientific arguments and your writing skills to increase in sophistication.

....

3 WHAT IS A SOCIAL SCIENCE ESSAY?

....

- The structure of a basic social science essay
- What is distinctive about a social science essay?
- Three golden rules for writing a social science essay

....

In the previous section we explored the various criteria that can be said to comprise an effective essay in the social sciences. In this section we consider what is distinctive about essay writing in the social sciences and what social science essays look like.

3.1 The structure of a basic social science essay

There are different types of social science essays, and essays of different lengths require slightly different approaches (these will be addressed later). However, all social science essays share a basic structure. At its simplest, a social science essay looks something like this:

- *Title*
  Every essay should begin with the title written out in full.
- *Introduction*
  The introduction tells the reader what the essay is about.
- *Main section*
  This section develops the key points of the argument in a 'logical progression'.

It uses evidence from research studies (empirical evidence) and theoretical arguments to support these points.
- *Conclusion*
The conclusion reassesses the arguments in order to make a final statement in answer to the question.
- *List of references*
This lists full details of the publications referred to in the text.

3.2   What is distinctive about a social science essay?

As you are no doubt aware, essay writing is a common feature of undergraduate study in many different subjects. What, then, is distinctive about essay writing in the social sciences? There are particular features that characterize social science essays and that relate to what is called the *epistemological* underpinning of work in this area (that is, to ideas about what constitutes valid social scientific knowledge and where this comes from). Among the most important of these characteristics are:

- the requirement that you support arguments with *evidence*, particularly evidence that is the product of systematic and rigorous research (see Section 7.2);
- the use of *theory* to build explanations about how the social world works (see Section 7.2).

Evidence is important in social scientific writing because it is used to support or query beliefs, propositions or hypotheses about the social world. Let's take a specific example. A social scientist may ask: 'Does prison work?'. This forms an initial *question*. To answer this question, the social scientist will need to formulate a more specific *claim*, one that can be systematically and rigorously explored. Such a claim could be formulated in the following terms: 'Imprisonment reduces the likelihood of subsequent

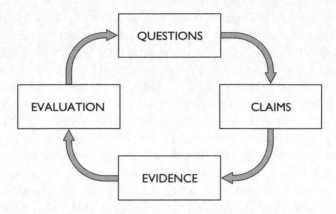

Figure 1   *The circuit of social scientific knowledge*
Source: Sherratt et al., 2000, p.18

reoffending'. This claim can now be subjected to systematic research. In other words, the social scientist will gather *evidence* for and against this claim, evidence that she or he will seek to interpret or *evaluate*. This process of evaluation may tend to support or refute the original claim, it may be inconclusive, and/or it may generate further questions. Together, these processes of enquiry can be described as forming a 'circuit of social scientific knowledge'. This circuit can be represented as in Figure 1.

Clearly, when writing undergraduate essays, it is not often (if at all) that you will be asked to conduct your own research. Generally, the expectation is that you will identify and evaluate evidence from existing research findings. However, the principle holds good, that when writing essays, social scientific claims have to be tested against the available evidence.

Theory is important in social scientific writing because the theoretical orientation of the social scientist will tend to inform the types of question she or he asks, the specific claims tested, the ways in which evidence is identified and gathered, and the manner in which this evidence is interpreted and evaluated. In other words, the theoretical orientation of the social scientist is liable to impact upon the forms of knowledge she or he will produce.

Take, for example, the research question we asked above, 'Does prison work?'. A pragmatic, policy-oriented social scientist may seek to answer this question by formulating a specific claim of the sort we identified, 'Imprisonment reduces the likelihood of reoffending'. She or he may then gather evidence of reoffending rates among matched groups of convicted criminals, comparing those who were imprisoned with those who were given an alternative punishment such as forms of community service. Evidence that imprisonment did not produce significantly lower rates of reoffending than punishment in the community may then be interpreted as suggesting that prison does not work, or that it works only up to a point. However, a Marxist social scientist may look at the same research findings and come up with a different conclusion, namely that the apparent failure of prison to reduce re-offending demonstrates that its primary purpose is not to reduce crime in the first place. Indeed, Marxist social scientists have argued that the growth of prisons in the nineteenth century was part of a much wider class struggle in which an emergent capitalist class sought to 'educate' the working class into forms of 'disciplined' behaviour necessary for factory labour.

The issue here is not whether the Marxist argument is right or wrong but that the theoretical orientation of the social scientist will inform how she or he evaluates the available evidence. Indeed, it is likely that a Marxist social scientist would have formulated an entirely different research 'claim' from the pragmatic or policy-oriented social scientist. For example, rather than seeking to test the claim, 'Imprisonment reduces the likelihood of reoffending', the Marxist social scientist may have sought to test the proposition, 'Prisons reproduce capitalist social relations'. The point for you to take away from this discussion is, then, that the theories we use shape the forms of social scientific knowledge we produce (see Figure 2).

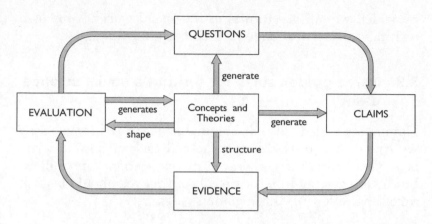

Figure 2 *Concepts and theories shape, and are shaped by,*
the circuit of knowledge
Source: adapted from Sherratt et al., 2000, p.18

There is considerable debate within the social sciences
about the exact relationship between theory and evidence.
To simplify somewhat, some social scientists tend to argue
that evidence can be used to validate or invalidate the
claims investigated by research and thereby produce
theoretical accounts of the social world that are more or
less accurate. Other social scientists will tend to argue that
our theoretical orientations (and the value judgements and
taken-for-granted assumptions that they contain) shape
the processes of social scientific enquiry to such an extent
that we can never claim to produce a straightforwardly
'accurate' account of the social world. Instead, they suggest
that social scientific knowledge is always produced from a
particular standpoint and will inevitably reflect the
assumptions of this.

Some of the implications of these points are discussed
further in Section 7.2, 'Using evidence to support your
argument'. For now, what you need to grasp is that essay
writing in the social sciences is distinguished by its
emphasis on the use of research evidence to support arguments and its emphasis on theory as central to the process

by which we build accounts of the social world. Your own writing will need to engage with both elements.

3.3 Three golden rules for writing a social science essay

Having identified what distinguishes a social science essay we can return to the more practical task of how to write one. This process is elaborated in the sections that follow, but before getting into the details of this you should bear in mind the following three golden rules.

Rule 1:   Write your answer in your own words

It's important to write in your own words because this is the best way in which you can come to understand a topic, and the only way of demonstrating this understanding to your tutor. How to avoid 'plagiarism' (or copying what someone else has already written or said) is dealt with in detail in Section 10.1. The important point to remember is that if you do plagiarize, your essay risks receiving a fail grade. You must therefore always put arguments in your own words except when you are quoting someone directly (in which case you must use the appropriate referencing conventions, discussed in Section 9 and Appendix D). The positive side of this seemingly draconian rule is that you will remember better what you have put in your own words. This ensures that you have the fullest understanding possible of the course. If there is an end-of-course exam, such an understanding is a real asset when it comes to revision.

Rule 2:   Answer the question that is asked

You will be surprised how easy it is to get this wrong. Most obviously, there is always the risk of misreading the question (suggestions on how to avoid this can be found in

Section 5.2). However, it is frequently the case that questions will 'index' a wider debate and will want you to review and engage with this. Thus, you need to avoid the danger of understanding the question but failing to connect it to the debate and the body of literature to which the question refers (this point is discussed more fully in 'Highlighting major debates and signposting the content of the argument' in Section 6.1). Equally, particularly on more advanced undergraduate courses, you are likely to be asked to work from an increasing range of sources. The dangers here include failing to select the most relevant material, selecting the less rather than the more relevant material, and failing to reorganize the material in a way that best fits the question.

Make sure that you take time to read the question properly to ensure that you understand what is being asked. Next, think carefully about whether there is a debate that 'lies behind' the question. Finally, identify the material that addresses the question most fully.

Rule 3: Think about content, structure and social scientific skills

You won't need to be told that the content of your essay needs to address material that is relevant to the question. However, structure and use of social scientific skills are also important. An effective structure is significant because the person who marks your essay will need to understand what is going on, so be considerate – a list of unconnected ideas and examples is likely to confuse, and will certainly fail to impress. The simplest way to avoid this is to follow the kind of essay writing conventions outlined in later sections of this guide. Social scientific skills (such as using theory and evidence, handling social scientific concepts and vocabulary, and evaluating competing arguments) are important because these indicate your ability to work creatively with the tools of the social scientist's trade.

....

Summary

- A basic social science essay has the following: a title, an introduction, a main section, a conclusion, and a list of references.
- Essays in the social sciences are distinguished by their emphasis on the use of evidence to evaluate arguments and the use of theory to build accounts of the social world.
- There is some debate in the social sciences on the relationship between theory and evidence.
- There are three golden rules of essay writing:
  1 Write your answer in your own words.
  2 Answer the question that is asked.
  3 Think about structure and social scientific skills as well as content.

....

4 MATCHING THE ANSWER TO THE QUESTION

....

- Answering advocacy questions
- Answering evaluation questions
- Answering compare and contrast questions

....

Many social science essay questions ask you to consider one or more positions that you are then required to advocate, evaluate, or compare and contrast.

4.1 Answering advocacy questions

Advocacy questions

Advocacy questions ask you to outline or explain and illustrate a particular issue, topic or argument. Examples of this kind of question would include:

- How have changes to the way in which the production of food is organized affected both the UK and other parts of the world? Illustrate your answer with relevant examples.
- 'An efficient allocation of resources requires fiscal neutrality, yet the British tax system persists in encouraging some activities while discouraging others.' Explain and illustrate with examples.
- Why can the changing politics of the UK not be understood unless they are set in a global context?
- What are the basic assumptions about humanistic psychology? How are these reflected in methods for encouraging growth?

Advocacy answers

A basic answer to an advocacy question might look something like this:

Introduction

Main section

- Provide a brief overview of the issue, topic or argument.
- Provide a more detailed breakdown of the key components of the issue, topic or argument.
- Give examples to illustrate these points.
- Briefly explore weaknesses in the viewpoint that you've been asked to advocate. Indicate alternative ways of thinking about the issues.

Or, as another example, you may decide to do the following:

- Provide a brief overview of the issue, topic or argument.
- Then, in more detail:
  outline one component of the issue, topic or argument and illustrate with an example;
  outline the second component of the issue, topic or argument and illustrate with another relevant example;
  outline the third component, . . . etc.
- Briefly explore weaknesses in the approach and indicate alternative ways of addressing the issues.

The material and the nature of the question will dictate the exact structure of an advocacy answer. When planning and drafting your essay, you should shift your argument around to identify what works best.

Conclusion

- Recap key points and illustrations. Give a final assessment of the usefulness of the approach.

Remember, this is only a basic format covering the major ingredients of an advocacy question and you shouldn't follow it slavishly.

Advocacy questions in relation to 'introductory', 'intermediate' and 'advanced' essay writing

Advocating a position is one of the more basic under-graduate essay writing skills. As you develop 'intermediate' and 'advanced' skills, you will be expected to show an increasing ability to outline and illustrate more complex positions, a greater understanding of their potential weak-nesses, and an increased awareness of alternative ways of addressing the issues.

4.2 Answering evaluation questions

Evaluation questions

In contrast to advocacy questions, evaluation questions ask you to explore arguments for and against a particular position or issue and to evaluate their relative strengths and weaknesses. Examples of this kind of question would include:

- To what extent does citizenship depend on having a modern welfare state?
- 'Conceptual categories are clearly defined and tightly structured as hierarchically organized mental repre-sentations.' How far do you agree with this view?
- Critically evaluate the definition of work as paid employment.
- Evaluate evidence in support of theories of working memory and levels of processing. What are the impli-cations for the modal model of memory?

Evaluation answers

A basic answer to an evaluation question might look something like this:

Introduction

Main section

- Outline the position.
- Give arguments (i.e. chains of logical reasoning) and evidence in support of the position.
- Give arguments supported by evidence that go against, question or limit the position.
- Weigh up the arguments for and against the position.

In the light of different material and different questions you may well want to adapt this basic format. For instance:

- You might start with the 'weaker' of the two arguments in the main section and follow it up with 'stronger' arguments. Will this convince the reader of your point of view more effectively?
- Rather than exploring the first position (a) then the second and competing position (b), you could explore one point from position (a) and contrast it with a parallel point from position (b), then explore another point from position (a) and contrast it with another point from position (b), and so on. Does this clarify or confuse your overall argument?

As with answers to advocacy questions, you will need to decide how best to structure the argument in the light of the question asked and the material used to answer it. Equally, you will need to emphasize different sections (the exploration of arguments for and against, the evaluation section) depending on the nature of the question.

The trick is to adapt this basic structure to a shape that best fits your requirements.

Conclusion

- Summarize, making an explicit statement as to which position (if any) you support.

Evaluation questions in relation to 'introductory', 'intermediate' and 'advanced' essay writing

Although perhaps more challenging than a basic advocacy question, evaluation is also a basic undergraduate essay writing skill. As you develop 'intermediate' and 'advanced' skills you will be expected to show an increasing ability to compare and contrast more complex positions, greater sophistication in your analysis of their strengths and weaknesses, increased awareness of alternative ways of addressing the issues, and more confidence in showing a reasoned preference for one position over another. Additionally, although not in all circumstances, you will be expected to demonstrate the ability to write from 'within' a perspective or theory. This means, on the basis of an informed academic judgement, adopting the conceptual world-view of a perspective or theory and evaluating competing perspectives and theories through the 'lens' of this world-view (see Section 7.2 below).

4.3 Answering compare and contrast questions

Compare and contrast questions

Compare and contrast questions ask you: to outline points of common ground between competing positions; to explore ways in which they differ, identifying how different positions often appeal to different kinds of evidence; and, sometimes, to compare the particular positions to other positions in the same field. Examples of this kind of question would include:

- Compare and contrast two different explanations of 'racial' divisions.
- Compare and contrast the views of Piaget and Mead on children's ability to take perspectives other than their own.
- In what ways do monetarist approaches differ from Keynesian approaches to the management of the UK economy? Are there any areas of agreement between them?

Compare and contrast answers

A basic answer to a compare and contrast question might look something like this:

Introduction

Main text

- Outline position (a) and position (b).
- Identify key points of common ground between these positions and compare them.
- Identify supplementary points of common ground between these positions and compare them.
- Identify and explore key points of contrast between position (a) and position (b).
- Identify and explore supplementary points of contrast between position (a) and position (b).
- If necessary, identify and explore significant ways in which position (a) and position (b) can be contrasted to a third competing position (c).
- Briefly evaluate the merits of these positions.

Once again, you will almost certainly need to adapt this basic format to fit different questions and different material. For instance:

- There may be an obvious debate 'behind' the question that requires you to emphasize the ways in which two contrasting positions share a common orientation that is in competition with a third position. This might be the case in the third of the example questions. It read: 'In what ways do monetarist approaches differ from Keynesian approaches to the management of the UK economy? Are there any areas of agreement between them?' Here you might need to emphasize that Keynesian and monetarist approaches share a common belief in the efficacy of the capitalist market that is in strong contrast to Marxist approaches. A debate of this kind may, then, require you to scale down the extent to which you compare and contrast positions (a) and (b) in order for you to contrast them to a third position (c).

- Equally, you may decide to compare a key point from positions (a) and (b) and then move straight on to contrast a key point from each position. You would then compare another point and contrast another point, and so on. This would be an alternative to exploring all the points of comparison in one section and then all the points of contrast in another. Ask yourself which method works best in relation to the question set and the material with which you are working.

As before, the trick is to adapt this basic structure to a shape that best fits your requirements.

Conclusion

- Summarize the major points of comparison and contrast between the positions and briefly recap which is the most persuasive and why.

Compare and contrast questions in relation to 'introductory', 'intermediate' and 'advanced' essay writing

Like advocacy and evaluation, comparing and contrasting is a basic undergraduate essay writing skill. As you develop 'intermediate' and 'advanced' skills you will be expected to show: an increasing ability to compare and contrast more complex positions; a greater sophistication in your analysis and a greater ability to emphasize key points; a greater confidence in showing a reasoned preference for one position over another; the ability to write from 'within' one position; and an increasing ability to relate the positions under analysis to relevant alternative positions in the same field.

....

Summary

- Advocacy questions ask you to outline and illustrate a particular issue, topic or argument.
- Evaluation questions ask you to explore arguments for and against competing positions and to evaluate their relative strengths and weaknesses.
- Compare and contrast questions ask you to identify and explore points of comparison and contrast between competing positions.
- These basic structures should be adapted in the light of the question and the material under discussion.
- As you develop 'intermediate' and 'advanced' skills you will be expected to show greater confidence and ability in deploying essay structuring skills. Your essay structures will need to demonstrate a developing complexity and comprehensiveness, giving due weight to relevant aspects of the argument.

....

5 STAGES OF WRITING FROM PREPARATION TO FINAL VERSION

....

- Use feedback and guidance notes
- Read the question
- Identify and organize the relevant material
- First draft to final version

....

Thorough preparation and planning is the basis of any good piece of written work, and it really is worth putting some effort into it. Here are some reminders for those of you already experienced in essay planning, and some suggestions for anyone coming to social science essay writing for the first time. (Bear in mind also the three golden rules for essay writing in Section 3.3 above.)

5.1 Use feedback and guidance notes

Try to make effective use of any sources provided that may help you tackle the essay question.

- If this is not your first essay, and if you haven't done so already, take a look at the previous essay you wrote. Did your tutor make any suggestions that you need to bear in mind for the forthcoming essay? Did you learn anything else about essay writing? Note down these points. (A checklist of activities for what to do when your essay is returned to you is given in Appendix A.)

- If there are guidance notes provided for you that relate to the essay question (these are always prepared for OU students), make sure you read them carefully.

5.2 Read the question

- Identify the process or 'command' words (for example, 'discuss', 'evaluate', 'explore'). These tell you *how* you have to answer the question. A list of these words and relevant definitions for each are in Appendix B.
- Identify the 'content' words. These tell you *what* you have to write about.

Let's consider the question:

'The family in Britain is in crisis.' Discuss.

'Discuss' is the command word (implying that you have to explore the evidence for and against the statement), and 'family', 'Britain', and 'crisis' are the content words. So, the evidence that you need to explore should focus on whether there is a crisis in the family in Britain and what 'crisis' might mean in this context.

5.3 Identify and organize the relevant material

- Read through any existing notes that you have, read or reread the sources specified for this particular essay and note all relevant material.

Having identified the relevant material, you will need to organize this into a shape that addresses the question. Here are some suggestions for tackling this task.

- First, 'wordstorm' your ideas for the essay on paper (that is, jot down a list of questions and issues prompted by the question, all the relevant examples you can think of, and any other related evidence); recheck notes and add left-out material; then link connected ideas and points. (Appendix C has examples of one way of doing this called 'mind maps'.)

- Collate and write out these points on separate sheets of paper, on 'post-its', or on index cards.
- Shuffle these until you've got them in a logical order (Section 7.1 offers ideas for creating a 'logical progression' in your argument). This is your essay plan.
- Ideas may come to you at unexpected moments – for these keep a notebook handy and jot them down.

If you have a word processor, you may want to do some of this on your screen.

5.4 First draft to final version

- Working from your essay plan, begin writing a first draft. You may need to revise your plan as the essay takes shape. Don't worry, this is perfectly normal!
- It may help to write out the question at the beginning of your first draft so that you keep its exact wording in front of you to ensure you are answering the question that is asked.
- Do the best you can, but see it as a first draft and expect to make some improvements – you may even want to prepare a second draft – before writing the final version.
- We all know that people sometimes hand in their first draft. If you have time, always put the essay aside for at least a day to let the dust settle, show it to a friend or another student to get feedback, and then reread the question and the essay yourself. Its strengths and weaknesses should now be a lot clearer to you.
- You're now in a position to write your definitive answer, and this is the time to consider more carefully

your presentation (sentence structure, grammar, etc.) and to check for clarity of expression.
- When this is complete, submit the essay and wait for feedback with quiet confidence.

The following sections of this guide offer more detailed help through the process of first attempt to final version – in short, writing your essay!

....

Summary

- Make use of sources of guidance.
- Essay writing has six principal stages:
    reading and understanding the question,
    identifying the relevant material,
    making an essay plan,
    writing a first draft,
    reviewing the first draft, maybe writing a second draft,
    writing a final version.

....

6   WRITING INTRODUCTIONS

....

- Longer or 'full' introductions
- Basic short introductions
- When do you write the introduction?

....

There are, of course, many ways to write an essay introduction. In this section, we will be exploring one of these, an
approach that treats the introduction like an 'abstract' or
brief synopsis of the central points raised in the essay. While
this is an effective and frequently used style of introduction,
you should not feel obliged to follow these guidelines
slavishly. Indeed, there is a danger that too rigid an inter-
pretation of the advice in this section will cause your
introductions to become dry and formulaic. As such, they
may fail to grab your reader's attention. Academic writers
often attempt to avoid this problem by, for example,
beginning an article or chapter with an arresting quotation,
image or challenging statement. Alternatively, they may
start with a short discussion of an example or theme central
to the matter in hand and use this to raise or 'signpost' the
questions to be addressed in the work that follows. You may
want to look for these and similar strategies in your reading.

  Having said this there are good reasons to develop
skills in writing the 'synopsis' style of introduction. The
introduction-as-synopsis will cover just about everything
that an effective introduction should achieve and will do
this using a minimum number of words, an important
consideration when the number of words available to you is
limited. Our advice is to ensure that you can write effective
introductions using the synopsis format and then, if you
wish, start to adapt this in more creative ways.

Like other areas of essay writing, you will probably find that you get better at introductions the more experienced you become. It is certainly fair to say that questions at more advanced levels will expect more from your introductions than questions at the introductory level. An introductory level essay should be able to identify the essay's subject and begin to highlight its key themes or arguments. More advanced essays should aim to display a firm grasp of the central debates that lie 'behind' the question and provide a sophisticated version of the author's own arguments. Sometimes more advanced essays will also need to 'establish a position' in the introduction, indicating that they are being written from 'within' a particular theory or perspective. This section explores all these issues by looking in depth at:

- longer or 'full' introductions for essays of over 1,500 words;
- basic short introductions for essays of between 1,000 and 1,500 words.

6.1 Longer or 'full' introductions

Full introductions can be written as a section in their own right and, in certain circumstances, may well be several paragraphs long. As a rough guide, a full introduction should be 5 to 10 per cent of your total word count.

'Full' introductions generally do most of the following: identify the subject of the essay; signpost the shape and content of the argument; highlight the major debates that lie 'behind' the question; define terms; and (sometimes) establish a position. We consider each of these features in more detail below.

Identifying the subject of the essay

The easiest way to do this is to refer back to the question. Let's take an example from everyday life (an example treated in more depth is in Essay 1 in Section 11). For instance, if the essay question states, 'Evaluate the claim that *Coronation Street* is the most enjoyable contemporary British soap opera', you may want to write:

> This essay will evaluate the claim that *Coronation Street* is the most enjoyable contemporary British soap opera.

However, you can always be more creative than this. For example, you might write:

> *Coronation Street* consistently receives high viewer-ratings. This essay explores the basis of this popularity, evaluating its appeal in comparison to two other major contemporary British soap operas: *EastEnders* and *Brookside*.

Signposting the shape of the argument

The intention here is to give the reader a 'road map' of the essay. At its simplest this involves highlighting the main stages of your argument. For instance, you might write:

> The first section focuses on . . . This argument is developed in the following section which explores . . .

Identifying the shape of your argument in this manner is called 'signposting'.

Highlighting major debates and signposting the content of the argument

Essay questions will often centre on a key debate or debates; for example, 'Does the First World exploit the Third World?' or 'Is behaviour biologically or socially produced?'. Often these debates will not be referred to explicitly but will lie 'behind' or be implied in the question asked. Your introduction will need to pull out these debates and signpost your essay's responses to them. This will form the core of your argument. For instance, in the case of the *Coronation Street* example, it may be possible to argue that, historically, *Coronation Street* has emphasized a less naturalistic style than either *EastEnders* or *Brookside*, one characterized by strong female characters and comic men. One of the debates lying 'behind' the question may then centre on the issue of whether *Coronation Street*'s less naturalistic style is more appealing to audiences or whether people are more drawn in by the focus on big social issues in *EastEnders* and *Brookside*. Your introduction could therefore refer to this debate. It might look like this:

> *Coronation Street* consistently receives high viewer ratings. This essay explores the basis of this popularity, evaluating its appeal in comparison to two other major contemporary British soap operas: *EastEnders* and *Brookside*. In the process, the essay will analyse *Coronation Street*'s use of strong female characters, its exploration of women's lives, and its humorous treatment of male characters. It will contrast these to the 'gritty realism' favoured by *EastEnders* and *Brookside*.

You will see that this introduction not only discusses *Coronation Street*'s style in opposition to the 'gritty realism' of *EastEnders* and *Brookside*, but also suggests that its appeal lies in its strong women characters and humorous treatment of men. In doing this, it signposts the content of the essay's argument, namely that *Coronation Street*'s less naturalistic style focuses on strong women characters and the humorous treatment of men, and that this is a core reason underpinning its popularity.

Defining terms

People can often be over-enthusiastic about defining terms. You don't need to define absolutely everything, particularly terms that are in widespread everyday use. Nevertheless, definitions can be useful in relation to the following:

- *Key concepts and obviously technical terms*
  For example, if you are asked to assess critically a particular theory or concept (say, the notion of globalization, the cultural imperialism thesis or cognitive developmental theory), it is fairly obvious that you will need to provide a definition or outline of it. In fact, it may be that this definition or outline will require several sentences and will look over-long and clumsy if included with your other introductory remarks. In consequence, you may decide that it is more appropriate to allot it a section of its own, perhaps immediately after the introduction proper.
- *Terms that are contested*
  For instance, the question 'Is the family in Britain in crisis?' hinges upon how you define 'crisis'. For some people factors such as the rising post-war divorce rate, increased numbers of lone-parent families and the increasing profile of feminism and lesbian and gay relationships constitute a 'crisis'. Other people find these developments positive or less problematic. Here you would need to point to the contested nature of the term and highlight the fact that it is open to competing definitions.
- *Theories or approaches that have different versions*
  Particularly on more advanced undergraduate courses where there is a greater emphasis on theoretical complexity, you will need to define the particular version of the theory or approach that you are using. For example, it may not be enough to say that you will use a 'Marxist analysis', because there are competing versions of Marxist theory.

Establishing a position

Establishing a position means indicating the particular
'line' that you intend to take in an essay. The statement,
'This essay explores the use of capital punishment in the
USA', certainly tells us what the essay is about. However,
the statement, 'This essay explores the use of capital
punishment in the USA and argues that it is a fundamental abuse of human rights', clearly establishes the
author's position on this issue and anticipates or signals
the content of the essay's conclusion. This helps orientate
the reader in the essay's argument and ensures that the
main point is lodged in her or his mind.

What would our *Coronation Street* example look like if
we included a statement that identified our position?
Perhaps something like this:

> *Coronation Street* consistently receives high viewer-
> ratings. This essay explores the basis of this popularity,
> evaluating its appeal in comparison to two other major
> British soap operas, *EastEnders* and *Brookside*. In its
> opening section, the essay uses feminist theory to
> analyse *Coronation Street*'s appeal in terms of its
> historical 'women centredness', in particular its focus on
> strong female characters, its exploration of women's
> lives and its often humorous treatment of men. The
> essay then goes on to contrast this approach to the more
> naturalistic 'gritty realism' of *EastEnders* and *Brook-
> side* which, it will be argued, have historically tended to
> focus more strongly on social issues such as unemploy-
> ment and HIV. The essay argues that, in comparison to
> *Coronation Street*, this 'gritty realism' fails to connect
> with women's culture and that it is the appeal to women
> of these less naturalistic elements that underlies
> *Coronation Street*'s continuing popularity.

The 'position' established here is a feminist one. In other
words, we are indicating that we will make a feminist
reading of soap opera.

6.2   Basic short introductions

In a very short essay you may only have between 50 and 100 words to tell your reader what the essay is about. As a result, your introduction will need to be concise and highly focused. It should still:

- identify the subject of the essay and define key terms;
- highlight any major debates that lie 'behind' the question;
- signpost the essay's key argument.

'I cut out only necessary words.'

However, it would probably stop there. Thus a short introduction to the same question, 'Evaluate the claim that *Coronation Street* is the most enjoyable contemporary British soap opera', might now read:

Coronation Street consistently receives high viewer ratings. This essay explores the basis of this popularity, evaluating its appeal in comparison to two other major contemporary British soap operas: *EastEnders* and *Brookside*. In the process, the essay will analyse *Coronation Street*'s use of strong female characters, its exploration of women's lives, and its humorous treatment of male characters. It will contrast these with the 'gritty realism' favoured by *EastEnders* and *Brookside*.

Outlining the content of your core argument will alert your reader to what is most important about the essay, or what makes it 'hang together'.

6.3   When do you write the introduction?

The difficulty with introduction writing is that sometimes you only know what the core arguments are when you have finished your essay. So, although writing the introduction can help to give you a clear idea of what you are doing, you may find that it is a good idea to write it last, that is, in your final version (though you will often find that you can also write a good introduction at second draft stage). If you have access to a word processor you can, of course, do this on screen at any stage.

An example of a formal social science essay introduction can be found in Essay 1, Section 11. You may want to compare this to the introduction of Essay 2 (also in Section 11). In what ways is the introduction to Essay 1 more effective?

....

Summary

- Introductions tell the reader what your essay is about. You may write it first to give you an idea of what you are doing, or you may find that you can write a better introduction when you have completed the main bulk of your essay.

- There is more than one way to write an introduction. The approach adopted here treats the introduction as an 'abstract' or synopsis of key points.
- 'Full' introductions: identify the subject of the essay; signpost the shape of the argument; highlight the major debates that lie 'behind' the question; signpost the content of the argument; (where necessary) define terms; (sometimes) establish a position or look ahead to the conclusion.
- A basic short introduction should tell the reader what the essay is about by: identifying the subject of the essay; highlighting the major debates that lie 'behind' the question; and identifying the essay's key argument(s) or theme(s).
- An introduction written to 'introductory' standards should be proficient at identifying the subject of the essay and signposting the shape of the argument.
- An introduction written to an 'intermediate' standard should move towards highlighting the major debates raised by the essay question, signposting the content of the argument, (if necessary) defining terms effectively, and (if appropriate) establishing a position.
- An introduction written to an 'advanced' standard should show greater sophistication in bringing out the major debates raised by the question, signposting the content of the argument, (if necessary) defining terms, and (if appropriate) establishing a position.
- Introductions should normally be between 5 and 10 per cent of the total length of the essay.
- Essays 1 and 2 in Section 11 illustrate stronger and weaker introductions.

....

7 WRITING THE MAIN SECTION

....

- Structuring your argument
- Using evidence to support your argument
- Adding weight to your argument
- Communicating your argument

....

Before you begin drafting your main section you may find it helpful to look back at Section 4, 'Matching the answer to the question', particularly the guidance on how to make your main section address appropriately the type of question you are answering.

7.1 Structuring your argument

Your essay needs a strong and coherent structure if you are to convince your reader of your case. Central to this is the process of building an argument, that is, making each point follow on from the previous one. It has been argued that creating a logical progression to a social scientific argument is not dissimilar to the way we argue in everyday life. In the example below, the author imagines what may be said in a discussion about whether it is better to shop at Waitrose rather than Sainsbury's. This is his answer (which he stresses is not intended to bear any relation to the facts):

'I think you'd be better off shopping at Waitrose.'

'It's a lot more convenient than Sainsbury's and they have a wider range of goods and the stuff's better quality. Their staff always seem to know the store inside out and can tell you whether or not they stock a particular item and what shelf it's on. And they're a lot friendlier there.'

'Waitrose is convenient because there are seldom long queues to wait in. That means you don't have to spend more time waiting to pay for your stuff than it took you to go around the store gathering it in.'

'My girlfriend likes chocolates, and Waitrose stock chocolates you've probably never heard of before. My girlfriend's always amazed at what I bring home.' Etc. Etc. . . .
(The Open University, 1994, p.35)

The author argues that if we look at this imagined reply carefully we can see a logical progression to it – that is, we can see the way it builds an argument. If we break it down, it looks something like this:

- *Outlines a particular point of view*
  'I think you'd be better off shopping at Waitrose.'

- *Gives reasons for holding this view*
  'It's a lot more convenient than Sainsbury's . . . they have a wider range of goods . . . the stuff's better quality', and so on.

- *Gives evidence (in an essay he might also cite theoretical arguments) to back up these claims*
  Waitrose is convenient because 'there are seldom long queues to wait in'; they have a wider range of goods because they 'stock chocolates you've probably never heard of'.

If you're the sort of person who likes diagrams you can represent the stages of this process as in Figure 3.

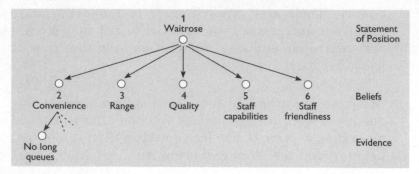

Figure 3 *'Waitrose vs. Sainsbury's' essay: logical
progression to argue Waitrose is best*
Source: The Open University, 1994, p.37

Of course, if this had been a formal essay, the writer
would have had to complete it with some kind of evaluation
(a section pointing to the limitations as well as the
strengths of his argument), together with a summary of
the main points.

If you now turn to Essay 1 in Section 11, you will find a
formal example of an essay that develops a logically
progressing argument. You may find it helpful to identify
the stages it goes through to build this argument (try this
for yourself).

If we 'strip down' the argument in Essay 1, we can see
that it goes through the following stages:

- First, it makes the claim that the social constructionist
  account is more persuasive than the alternative,
  biological account.
- Second, it identifies reasons to support this view (e.g.
  Butler's notion that sex/gender is a 'performative
  enactment'; Connell's argument that sex/gender is a
  relational category produced in a process of 'hegemonic'
  struggle).
- Third, it cites evidence from the sociological research
  literature on sex/gender and schooling to evaluate this
  argument.

Of course, the stages of the argument in Essay 1 are slightly more complicated than this. For instance, it uses Connell early on to question some aspects of the social constructionist case and then returns to these points in its conclusion. However, this basic structure can still be seen, as it were, beneath the surface of the essay.

....

Summary

- The argument in the main section of an essay needs to have 'logical progression'.
- We construct logically progressing arguments in everyday life.
- Logical progression involves: outlining a particular point of view; giving reasons why this point of view might be correct; and providing theoretical and empirical evidence to support these claims.

....

7.2 Using evidence to support your argument

More advanced undergraduate courses are likely to require you to draw on an increasing range of sources, including primary texts and other original material. Clearly, in handling this material, you will need to reorganize it in a way that answers the question. You will also need to select from it the evidence that most effectively supports your argument.

Selecting evidence – using a range of examples

Any essay question will expect you to support your arguments with appropriate examples and evidence. However, as you develop intermediate and advanced essay writing skills, you will be expected to demonstrate an increasing ability to select examples that illustrate and support your points most effectively. In general, you should:

- *Highlight examples that have the most significant or far-reaching implications.*
  The examples will need to be relevant to the question and engage with the point that you are making. This means being selective. You cannot cite every single related example or piece of evidence in the relevant literature. Some examples will be more useful to your purpose than others, and you will need to identify these and relate them to the issue under discussion.

- *Where possible, support your argument with more than one example.*
  This does not mean that you should use a number of examples to make the same point over and over again. Rather, we are suggesting that you will need to draw on a range of examples to illustrate the different aspects of your argument. However, you will sometimes need to decide whether it is more effective to explore an issue in depth or in breadth. For instance, exploring one or a limited range of examples in depth may allow you to provide a richer and more detailed account than exploring a breadth of examples only briefly. You will need to decide which strategy is most appropriate according to the question and the material available.

- *Select examples from a range of sources.*
  Particularly on more advanced undergraduate courses, you will need to look for a breadth of source material, thereby demonstrating your familiarity with the field. As well as the academic literature, it may be that up to the minute examples can be found in, for example, news and current affairs. Where such examples are effective in illuminating an academic argument they can be a useful addition to your essay.

- *Work from the general to the particular.*
  Specific examples should be used to support general arguments. Whereas a general argument cannot necessarily be induced from only one or two concrete examples, one or two concrete examples can be used to illustrate the truth of a general argument on the grounds that there are many more examples of the same point but it is not possible to cite them in your essay.

Advice for OU students

OU course materials provide a range of sources on which you can draw (for example, additional readings and set texts, cassettes, and television or video programmes). If you have access to other material that is relevant to your course, you may decide to draw on this. However, unless specified other-wise, you will not be required to use sources in addition to the course materials. Indeed, you should remember that you will be assessed primarily on your understanding of the given course content.

Essay 1 in Section 11 illustrates the use of examples to support an argument. You may want to try to identify these now for yourself.

As you will have seen, Essay 1 cites a range of examples from the research literature on sex/gender and schooling to support and illustrate what it identifies as the three major arguments to be found in this literature (that the content and practices of schooling encode sex/gender; that pupils actively use sex/gender to negotiate schooling; and that sex/gender relations intersect with other social relations in the school). It attempts to identify particularly 'rich' examples, to cite different sources, to indicate where similar data can be found in other research, and to work from the general to the particular. Now look at how Essay 2 builds an argument. Why is Essay 1 more successful in doing this?

Selecting evidence – using empirical evidence

In the preceding paragraphs we have discussed, in general terms, the use of examples as evidence. However, it is important to be clear that these examples will frequently be drawn from concrete research findings. Social scientists carry out research studies to gather evidence to substantiate or falsify their theories and arguments. Evidence from such research is called empirical evidence (loosely speaking, evidence collected via systematic and rigorous observation), and since it comes from checkable, usually published investigation it is more highly regarded than everyday examples or personal experience. As is the case with Essay 1, a good essay will use empirical evidence to support the arguments made. This involves more than simply describing relevant research findings. The task is to make clear exactly how these findings support or illustrate your arguments. For example, if you look at Essay 1 you will find the following paragraph:

> As well as producing sex/gender through friendship group interactions, the literature also suggests that pupils use sex/gender to negotiate and resist schooling. Kehily and Nayak (1996, p.214) describe an account from a group of secondary school pupils in which one of them (Samantha) was claimed to have pursued a teacher (Mr. Smedley) round the classroom with a sprig of mistletoe with the intention of 'getting some lipstick on the top of his head'. In this instance, a hetero-sexualized form of femininity is used satirically to undermine the authority of a male teacher (see, also, Walkerdine, 1981).

This paragraph:

- identifies the argument (that the social meanings and practices of sex/gender are used by pupils to negotiate and resist schooling);

- cites research evidence to support this claim (from Kehily and Nayak, 1996);
- explains exactly how this evidence illustrates the initial argument (it is an instance where femininity was used to undermine a male teacher's authority); and,
- provides an additional reference identifying further research findings supporting this argument (Walkerdine, 1981).

Selecting evidence – using maps, diagrams and numerical data

Maps, diagrams and numerical data are further major sources of evidence that you can use to illustrate and support your argument. Although the use of numerical data may not always be explicitly called for, you will always gain extra marks for judicial use of such data where relevant. Maps, diagrams and numerical data, rather like quotations, should be used to illustrate and support points in your argument and not to replace it, so always remember to integrate them into the points you are making.

If you reproduce maps, diagrams or numerical data you will need to give your sources for them. However, it is often sufficient to refer to them, for example, by saying 'As the data used by Smith show . . . (Smith, 2000, p.15, Table 1)', and providing a full reference at the end of your essay (references are dealt with in detail in Section 9 and Appendix D). In addition, remember that maps, tables and graphs are not hard facts. You will need to be critical of your sources by, for example, bearing in mind what scale is being used and how this shapes the evidence, by questioning how data have been collected, or by asking how a graph would change if plotted over a wider timescale. You should also be aware that numerical data represent specific outcomes and that the underlying causes of those outcomes will be unclear and will need further investigation. For example, it is quite possible for different combinations of causes to produce a similar numerical outcome.

Using theory, being 'critical'

Essay questions will often require you to explore theoretical arguments as well as concrete examples, and you will also want to draw on other people's theories as evidence to support your own argument. The ability to demonstrate an understanding of competing theoretical positions and to identify the fundamental strengths and weaknesses of each is a basic requirement of undergraduate essay writing. As you develop intermediate and advanced essay writing skills you will be expected to demonstrate the ability to understand and apply arguments from primary theoretical texts (as opposed to relying on commentaries on these), demonstrate an understanding of more complex theoretical positions, be more confident in expressing a reasoned preference for one theoretical position over another; and demonstrate the ability to write from 'within' a perspective or theory.

In working with theories remember that it is like looking through different pairs of spectacles – they make us see the world in different ways, such as in a Marxist way or in a feminist way. As a result, we have to accept that theories do not let us see the world 'as it is'; we see only what they allow us to see. In fact, as we saw in Section 3.2 above, many social scientists argue that you can never see the world 'as it is' and that you always have to look at it from one perspective or another. The task is to find a 'pair of spectacles' that allow us to view the object under study in as useful a way as possible. These points have some important implications:

- Competing theories are not all equal. Different theories appeal to different kinds of evidence. Different theories are 'useful' in different contexts.

- You cannot lump together the good bits of a whole range of theories to make one 'super theory'. Different theories will contradict each other. As a result, incorporating an insight from one theory into an existing approach will often require a radical restructuring of *both*.
- Even when you can make a new theory from aspects of previous ones, you still won't have a view of the world 'as it really is'. You may have a more powerful pair of spectacles to look through but you will still have to ask yourself the following questions: Is there something beyond the range of these spectacles that I can't see? Are these spectacles still obscuring what I can see? If I turn to look at a new object, do my spectacles work as well as they did when I looked at the first object? Asking these sorts of questions is called being 'critical'. This doesn't mean being negative about everything. It means 'standing outside' a theory, looking for its limitations as well as its strengths.

Essay 1 provides a formal example of an essay that demonstrates a systematic engagement with and evaluation of theoretical material. You may want to look, in particular, at the conclusion, where the author attempts to identify some of the limitations of the theoretical arguments in the literature on sex/gender and schooling. You may also want to compare the use of theoretical material in Essay 1 with that in Essay 2. In what ways is Essay 1 more effective in handling and applying theory?

Writing from 'within' a theory or perspective

At several points in the previous sections we have highlighted the importance of writing from 'within' a theory or perspective, particularly in the context of more advanced undergraduate courses. This refers to the ability to take on the conceptual world-view of a particular theoretical standpoint. Individual social scientists are generally identified as working within and contributing to particular theoretical traditions. For example, the work of Stuart Hall, Emeritus Professor of Sociology at the Open University, has been closely identified with a culturalist and post-structuralist rereading of the Italian Marxist, Antonio Gramsci. The work of Margaret Wetherell, Professor in Psychology at the Open University, is closely identified with a discursive approach to psychology. Like other social scientists, both Hall and Wetherell can be said to write from 'within' the conceptual universe of these specific perspectives. Their work is steeped in the histories of these perspectives; it reproduces and clarifies the perspectives' distinctive vocabularies and conceptual tools, and contributes to knowledge through applying these tools to new objects of enquiry and by questioning and pushing at the boundaries of their respective traditions.

The ability to write from within a perspective or theory can, then, be said to have at least two important aspects. First, it is a sign of increasing intellectual maturity. It demonstrates a familiarity with, and confidence in handling, the vocabulary and conceptual framework of a particular theoretical tradition. Second, it demonstrates the confidence to take sides in intellectual debates. The social scientist's duty to evaluate critically does not mean that we should adopt a uniform and bland relativism where all forms of knowledge are considered equally useful. The point of writing from 'within' a particular perspective or theory is that you are prepared to take a stand and say, 'This is useful knowledge'. This does not mean that you should attempt to shape evidence to fit a preconceived standpoint. It means taking an informed position on the basis of reasoned academic judgement and with due reference to the potential limits of your own arguments. An example of a student essay in which the author clearly writes from 'within' a perspective (social constructionism) and uses this to take up a firm position on the set question can be found in Essay 1 in Section 11.

However, it is worth stressing that essay questions will not of necessity require that you write from 'within' a perspective or theory. Indeed, they may specify that you should adopt an explicitly neutral position, standing 'outside' one or more positions in order to evaluate them critically. Equally, it will not always be possible to make a reasoned judgement between competing positions. After careful consideration, it may be the case that the explanations they offer are equally strong or equally weak. If this is the case, you should say so.

Being 'self-reflexive'

In the social sciences, choosing between competing theories or arguments will, at some point, involve making a value judgement. Although it may be possible to identify clear reasons why some arguments are more persuasive than others, our choice will almost inevitably be shaped by our political, moral and philosophical values. While not all social scientific writing will demonstrate this, it is good practice to make explicit the theoretical or political orientation that underpins your work rather than pretending that your argument is simply 'objective'. For example, you might indicate that the essay is being written from 'within' a feminist, or Foucauldian, or cognitive development perspective. This will alert readers to possible bias or areas of partiality in your argument and will allow them to make up their own minds about the strengths of your case. In fact, by signalling your possible blind spots to the reader, you are being more objective than if you pretended such blind spots did not exist. For example, in Essay 1 in Section 11 the author clearly indicates in the introduction that, on the basis of reasoned judgement, the essay is written from a position sympathetic to a particular theory ('social constructionism'). This alerts the reader to the potential bias in the subsequent material.

Summary

- As you progress to more advanced undergraduate courses you will increasingly be required to select relevant material from a range of sources and relate this back to the individual essay question.
- Arguments should be supported with appropriate illustrations and evidence. Try to select a range of the most significant examples – some are richer and more far-reaching than others. Examples should relate back to the essay question and engage with the argument that you are making.
- For some courses you will need to use maps, diagrams or numerical data. These should be used as evidence to support your argument, but remember, they are not 'hard facts'.
- Social science essays often ask you to explore theoretical arguments and use these as evidence as well as concrete examples. As you develop your essay writing skills you will need to show increasing confidence in exploring the strengths and weaknesses of competing theories.
- Some theories are stronger and more convincing than others; theories cannot necessarily be lumped together to make a 'super theory' – they often contradict each other. In handling theories, social scientists need to be 'critical', that is, they need to display an awareness of a theory's weaknesses and its strengths. However, one sign of increasing intellectual maturity is the ability to write from 'within' a perspective.
- Being 'self-reflexive' means acknowledging your own particular biases, for example, by indicating that you are arguing from a specific point of view.
- Many of these points are illustrated in Essay 1 in Section 11.

7.3   Adding weight to your argument

Social scientists highlight key works and use quotations for the following reasons:

- as a source of evidence, that is, to support and illustrate their own points;
- to provide the reader with a 'map' of the most important work done in the area under discussion;
- to demonstrate to the reader that they have thought about and understood what other people have written on a subject and that their own arguments should be taken seriously.

As you progress to more advanced undergraduate courses you should expect to demonstrate an increased ability to select appropriate quotations and cite key texts in order to add weight to your argument.

Let's take a brief look at some of these strategies in operation. Here is an example of one writer, the sociologist, Máirtín Mac an Ghaill, citing research evidence to support his argument and to map work in the field. He writes:

During the 1970s and 1980s, Irish community workers and academics brought together a wide range of empirical evidence of the institutional and individual discrimination that the Irish experience in a wide range of Britain's institutional sites, including migration, work, health, education, policing and legal systems and welfare rights (Conner 1985; Hickman 1986, 1995b; Hazelkorn 1990; Greenslade 1992; Gribben 1994; Kowarzik 1997; Williams et al., 1997). Most significantly, Mary Hickman and Bronwen Walter (1997) have recently carried out a large-scale empirical study, funded by the Commission for Racial Equality, entitled *Discrimination and the Irish Community in Britain*. As this work finely illustrates, one of the major effects of the black–white dualistic model of race and racism is that it does not help us to

understand the current high levels of disadvantage
experienced by the Irish in Britain.
(Mac an Ghaill, 1999, p.79)

In this passage, Mac an Ghaill maps existing research on
anti-Irish discrimination. However, he also uses what he
identifies as a key study (by Hickman and Walter) to
support his argument that conventional notions of racism
fail to address the experience of Irish people in Britain.

In the next extract, the feminist theorist, Chris
Weedon, uses an actual quotation to support her argument
that women's reproductive capacity is central to biological
theories of gender difference. She writes:

Biological theories of difference, from Darwin to
contemporary socio-biology, tend to focus on women's
and men's different reproductive roles. Motherhood as
the essence of woman's being was central to nine-
teenth- and early twentieth-century scientific accounts
of gender. . . . Here is an example from the widely read
'Self and Sex' series of books, published in . . . 1901 . . .

Let us consider a little, [woman's] peculiar adaptation, and the suitability of each part to the
purpose intended by the all-wise Creator. . . .
Unlike man in her physical form, her departure
from his type, was to fit her for motherhood.
Narrower shouldered and less muscular, because
not needing the brawn for lifting and labouring
with her hands in the harder coarser ways; she is
broader through the hips to give ample room for
cradling her children.
(Drake, 1901, pp.27–28)

(Weedon, 1999, pp.6–7)

There are several points that are worth pulling out of these
examples:

- In each case, the writers use their quotation or references to other authors to support a point that they themselves are making. This is important because there is a temptation to let quotations in particular do the work for you. Quotations and references to other people's work should support rather than replace your argument.
- Both writers are very careful to provide *references* for the works that they cite. We look at references in more detail later in Section 9.
- Weedon is very careful to *introduce* her quotation with the phrase, 'Here is an example . . .' Quotations that are not introduced in some way can read as if they have appeared out of nowhere and interrupt the 'flow' of the writing.
- Weedon has indented her quotation. All quotations need to be identified as such. It is usual to indent longer quotations to distinguish them from your own argument. Shorter quotations do not need to be indented, but need to be enclosed in single inverted commas.
- Shortening or adding to your quoted material needs to be shown. If you leave out irrelevant phrases, indicate such cuts with three dots (. . .) known as an ellipsis. Similarly, if you need to add or substitute a word or phrase to clarify the sense, put your inserted words in square brackets. For example, 'Let us consider a little, [woman's] peculiar adaptation.'

....

Summary

- Quotations and references to key texts are used: as a source of evidence; to provide the reader with a 'map' of the most important works in an area; and to give the work 'authority'.
- Quotations should be introduced.
- Longer quotations should be written in a separate paragraph indented at the left-hand (and sometimes right-hand) margins. Shorter quotations can be written

in the main text in single inverted commas. Any changes should be indicated.

• Quotations and key texts highlighted in an essay should be supported by a reference.

• As your skills develop, and certainly at intermediate standard, you should be able to select appropriate quotations and cite key texts in support of your argument.

....

7.4 Communicating your argument

You may feel happy that you have grasped the essay question and are able to answer it comprehensively and logically, but to prove this you will need to be able to convey your ideas, to communicate them to your reader.

'Well . . . er . . . this is it.'

Thinking about the audience

Students often ask who their reader is meant to be. Commonly, this reader is identified as the 'intelligent lay-person'. While this notion is useful, it presents problems in that even the intelligent lay-person cannot be expected to know much of the technical vocabulary that is taken for granted in the social sciences. Perhaps a more useful idea is to think of your reader as someone studying the social sciences at the same level as you but at another university. You can assume that your reader will have a grasp of basic social scientific ideas, so you won't need to explain every last detail to them. However, they won't necessarily be studying the same things as you are, so you will need to explain more complex ideas and be careful to define your terms. For the most advanced undergraduate courses you can assume that your reader will have a greater degree of sophistication and you can therefore afford to write with more complexity. In fact, by the end of advanced undergraduate courses you should probably aim to be writing for an expert audience.

Clear sentences and paragraphs

The general rule in essay writing is to keep your sentences simple and easily understood. However, like other academic fields, the social sciences tend to have formal written styles and specialized vocabularies. Social scientific vocabulary cannot be dismissed simply as 'jargon' (although sometimes this might be a justified criticism). Academic disciplines need a complex language to be able to deal with complex issues. Unfortunately, this may cause you problems. There is a real danger that in trying to sound 'academic' you may simply sound confused. Our advice is, if you are unsure, keep things simple. Even when you feel more confident you need to remember that there is nothing to be gained from using complex language for its own sake. The real test lies in being able to communicate complex ideas in the form that is most easily understood.

Equally, your paragraphs need to be as clear and straightforward as possible. The 'Rubin method' of paragraph analysis (Rubin, 1983) suggests that paragraphs have:

- a topic;
- a series of statements that explain what the author thinks is special or relevant about the topic;

and that, put together, these form the paragraph's

- main idea.

A 1,500-word essay is likely to have five or six key points as well as an introduction and conclusion. Each paragraph should address one key point or one aspect of a key point. You may want to try the Rubin method on the Mac an Ghaill and Weedon examples in the previous subsection. What is the 'main idea' in each?

Giving the essay direction

If readers are to avoid getting lost in your argument you need to tell them what is happening at key points along the way. There are three effective ways to do this:

- introduce and summarize the main sections;
- recap and signpost your argument;
- where useful, remind the reader of the subject of your essay.

These points are elaborated below but you can also see them applied in an actual essay in Essay 1 in Section 11.

Introducing and summarizing the main sections

To illustrate this point, here is an example from a reading by Gail Lewis, Senior Lecturer in Social Policy at the Open University. Lewis is exploring welfare policy and the social construction of 'race'. She has just argued that constructions of nation (who belongs, who doesn't) are intimately connected to social exclusion and she is moving on to explore education as another social site in which racialized social exclusions occur. This is how she handles the transition:

> In this section [I have] introduced . . . the link between 'race' and that of nation . . . In the following sections we will consider further the social exclusions which emerge as a result of 'race' and ethnicity. The focus will be on education but it is important to remember that this is not a chapter *about* education. Rather, we use education as a site of policy in order to illustrate the social construction of social difference.
>
> One place to begin looking at the complex interweaving of exclusions and inclusions is in the field of education in England and Wales.
> (Lewis, 1998, p.104)

If we break down this passage we can see Lewis doing the following:

- She first reiterates the key point from her previous discussion (the link between the idea of 'race' and that of nation), thus underscoring and concluding the argument of this section.
- She next creates a bridge between this first section and her new point ('In the following sections we will consider further the social exclusions which emerge as a result of 'race' and ethnicity . . .').
- Finally, she introduces her new section and signposts its content ('One place to begin looking at the complex

interweaving of exclusions and inclusions is in the field of education in England and Wales').

Recapping and signposting

Throughout her chapter, Lewis carefully recaps and signposts her argument as a means of binding the argument together. One frequently used device for signposting in the main text of an essay or academic article is to indicate that there are various issues that you aim to explore, and then to list these issues as you discuss them. For instance, Lewis adopts this strategy in her discussion of social exclusion, 'race' and nation. She writes:

> If the nation is imagined as being made up of people said to be the same colour and said to have the same ethnic origins, then all those who are defined as not meeting these two criteria can be constructed as being 'outside' the nation . . . So 'race' can be mapped on to 'the nation' to produce a structure for excluding groups of people either from entering the borders of the nation at all, or, if 'inside', from having access to the full range of [economic and welfare benefits]. This may be understood by thinking about the link between the structure and rules of immigration control and welfare benefits and services. There are three important points to note at the outset.
>
> First, the exclusion of racialized groups from access to welfare benefits and/or services goes back at least to the 1905 Aliens Act. . . .
>
> Second, since the 1960s, the treatment of black people in the UK, especially if they are poor, has been framed by a series of immigration and nationality laws and rules. These have had the effect of withdrawing or

restricting the rights of black Commonwealth citizens (and their descendants). . . .

Third, the exclusions on the basis of 'racial' categorization are not separate from the exclusions associated with class. . . .
(Lewis, 1998, pp.101–102)

Although we do not have space to include the full details of Lewis's argument, you can see from the above extract how she first signposts and then signals the three stages in her argument about how racialized constructions of nation impact on black people's access to welfare benefits and services. This strategy clearly helps the reader locate herself or himself in the ongoing discussion.

Having signposted the development of her argument, Lewis then concludes her discussion by recapping its core point. She writes:

Legislation has, then, progressively altered the terms on which black people from the Commonwealth can gain legal citizenship and this has the knock-on effect of excluding people from access to welfare services and benefits.
(Lewis, 1998, p.102)

By deploying these strategies of signposting and recapping, Lewis helps orientate the reader in her argument and successfully drives home the points she is seeking to make.

Referring back to the subject of the essay

This is the final strategy you can use to stop your reader getting lost in the argument. However, it is important not to be too laborious about this. For example, constantly repeating the essay title in full can sometimes sound clumsy. You don't necessarily want your essay peppered with phrases like 'In answering the question "Evaluate the importance of the unconscious in Freud's model of the mind" it is thus necessary to . . .'. You can often reference the subject of the essay more simply by picking out and reusing a key phrase. For instance, on page 102 of the previously discussed chapter, Lewis (1998) writes, 'Thus, there is a variety of ways in which social exclusion occurs'; and on page 103 she writes, 'In addition to the exclusions which arise from structural arrangements there are also exclusions which result from the ways in which things are described or seen'. Reiteration of the phrase 'social exclusion' serves to remind the reader what the chapter is about.

Making your essay 'flow'

Link words and sentences are used to make an essay 'flow', that is, they make the writing easy to read. Let's take a final look at an extract from Lewis's (1998) chapter on 'race' and social exclusion. Here she defines what she means by the term, 'social exclusion'.

> At a most basic level, to be excluded from something means being denied access to an activity, a place, or a range of resources. Apart from accident or oversight, such denials of access can be the result either of failure to meet specified conditions of entry, or of lack of financial resources. As such, exclusions can be the result of both formal and informal, direct and indirect, rules or arrangements. For example, to be denied access to something because you do not have the money required for entry is the result of indirect arrange-ments. This is because it is linked to the distribution of financial resources among a set of individuals and groups rather than because of the imposition of a set of rules or conditions.
> (Lewis, 1998, p.98)

Now reread the extract with all the link words and phrases removed.

> To be excluded from something means being denied access to an activity, a place, or a range of resources. Denials of access can be the result either of failure to meet specified conditions of entry, or of lack of financial resources. Exclusions can be the result of both formal and informal, direct and indirect, rules or arrangements. To be denied access to something because you do not have the money required for entry is the result of indirect arrangements. It is linked to the distribution of financial resources among a set of individuals and groups rather than because of the imposition of a set of rules or conditions.
> (adapted from Lewis, 1998, p.98)

Without the link words and phrases, the extract reads like a list of points or something written in note form, and the reader is jolted from one issue to another. In making sure that you link sentences and paragraphs, you thus ensure that your reader's attention sticks to the argument and doesn't get distracted by your writing.

....

Summary

- One way to think of your notional reader is as someone studying the social sciences at an equivalent level in another University. They will understand basic social scientific concepts but won't necessarily be familiar with the area addressed in your essay. By the end of advanced undergraduate courses you should aim to write for an 'expert' audience.
- The aim of (good) essay writing is to convey complex ideas in as clear a form as possible.
- Paragraphs contain a topic and a series of statements explaining what is relevant about this topic. Together

these make up its 'main idea'. A 1,500-word essay will have five or six key points plus an introduction and conclusion.

- You can give your essay a strong sense of direction by: introducing and summarizing main sections; recapping and signposting your argument; where useful, referring back to the question.
- Using link words and sentences ensures that your essay 'flows' smoothly.
- You can see these points applied to an actual essay in Essay 1 in Section 11.

8 WRITING CONCLUSIONS

....

- What a conclusion should aim to do
- What a conclusion should contain

....

Conclusions are an important part of an essay, and a well written conclusion is a good way of picking up extra marks.

8.1 What a conclusion should aim to do

The primary job of a conclusion is to provide a final condensed version of the essay's core argument and in the process to provide an overview of the state of 'current knowledge' or 'current opinion' on any one topic. Since your conclusion should take up no more than 10 per cent of your essay, a short essay (of 1,000 to 1,500 words) won't have room to do much more than this. However, if you are writing a longer essay (of 1,500 words and over) your conclusion should do the following:

- recap the key points in your argument/summarize the key debates raised by the question, and try to synthesize them;
- provide a final condensed version of the essay's core argument that restates your position on the question;
- if necessary, identify absences in your argument that could be explored in future work.

Put simply, a conclusion should leave the reader with a clear impression of your argument – what it was about, what you believe, and why you believe this. An introductory level essay is likely to demonstrate the ability to summarize content clearly and concisely. More advanced essays will be expected to progress towards writing more complex conclusions that emphasize condensed versions of your core argument.

8.2   What a conclusion should contain

If you have read the section on writing introductions, you will remember the following question and introduction:

> Evaluate the claim that *Coronation Street* is the most enjoyable contemporary British Soap opera.

> *Coronation Street* consistently receives high viewer-ratings. This essay explores the basis of this popularity, evaluating its appeal in comparison to two other major British soap operas, *EastEnders* and *Brookside*. In its opening section, the essay uses feminist theory to analyse *Coronation Street*'s appeal in terms of its historical 'women centredness', in particular its focus on strong female characters, its exploration of women's lives and its often humorous treatment of men. The essay then goes on to contrast this approach to the more naturalistic 'gritty realism' of *EastEnders* and *Brookside* which, it will be argued, have historically tended to focus more strongly on social issues such as unemployment and HIV. The essay argues that, in comparison to *Coronation Street*, this 'gritty realism' fails to connect with women's culture and that it is the appeal to women of these less naturalistic elements that underlies *Coronation Street*'s continuing popularity.

Imagine that we now have to write a conclusion to the same essay. We will have written a main section that develops these arguments and provides supporting evidence to back up and illustrate our claims. We now have to bring the essay to a close, leaving the reader with a clear overall impression of our argument and our reasons for holding this position. From the introduction it's clear that the main thrust of our argument is that *Coronation Street*'s appeal lies in the way it speaks to women's experiences and women's culture. As a result, we may well write a conclusion that looks something like the following:

> As I have shown, both *EastEnders* and *Brookside* have historically worked within a broadly naturalistic framework that emphasizes social diversity (for example, the lesbian and gay characters, the limited presence of black and other minority ethnic groups) and that prioritizes the treatment of 'difficult' social issues (for example, domestic violence, HIV, drug use and unemployment). These emphases constitute the programmes' often commented on, 'gritty realism'. We might assume that these emphases on naturalism and social diversity would guarantee the programmes' popular appeal. However, as the essay has argued, *Coronation Street*'s appeal appears to lie, at least in part, precisely in its use of a diluted naturalism. Despite recent examples of 'gritty realist' storylines (e.g. teenage pregnancy) it is arguable that *Coronation Street* remains far less concerned with representing a broad range of social issues and social groups, favouring instead an emphasis on strong female characters, storylines that explore women's experience, and a rich array of comic characters and comic situations, many of which are at the expense of men. As the essay has argued, these aspects of *Coronation Street* can be said to connect with women's culture. The programme's women-centredness can thus be seen as a central part of its continuing strong position in the television ratings war.

If we break down this conclusion into its component parts, we can see that it does the following:

- recaps the key stages in the argument/summarizes the key debates raised by the question (that is, the argument that *EastEnders* and *Brookside* favour 'gritty realism' while *Coronation Street* is less naturalistic but strongly women-centred);
- provides a final condensed statement of the essay's core argument (this women-centredness underlies its popular appeal).

This conclusion hasn't identified absences in the argument that could be explored in future work, and it isn't always necessary to do this. However, what if in the main section of the essay we had provided examples illustrating *Coronation Street*'s putative 'woman centredness', but had not established (via audience research) that this was what actually appealed to women viewers? In this case, our conclusion might suggest that further research was necessary to substantiate (or falsify) our hypothesis. This, then, is an absence in our argument that could be explored in future work.

The above is one conclusion that we might have written to this particular essay question. However, you might disagree with the argument and want to write something completely different. Equally, you could have expressed the same points in a number of different ways. Alternatively, you might feel that you couldn't write a conclusion like this because it is 'too complicated' or 'too well written'. If this is the case, don't worry. You could write a serviceable conclusion in a much simpler form. The point is that there is more than one way to write a conclusion, and you should not view this example as a template to be followed slavishly.

If you want to look at a more formal example of a social science essay conclusion, you should read Essay 1 in Section 11. Here the author summarizes the argument, while also taking a clear stand in relation to the question and indicating some possible limitations in the literature. Compare this to the conclusion of Essay 2. Why is Essay 1's conclusion more successful?

Summary

- The primary job of a conclusion is to provide a final condensed version of your essay's core argument and thereby to summarize the key debates raised by the question, or provide an overview of 'current knowledge' on a given topic.
- Longer conclusions should: recap the subject of the essay in some form; recap the key stages in the argument/ summarize the key debates raised by the question; provide a final condensed version of the argument that restates the essay's position on the question; (if necessary) identify absences in the argument that could be explored in future work.
- An essay written to an 'introductory' standard might be expected to provide a conclusion that demonstrates an ability to summarize the content of the essay clearly and concisely. More advanced essays should move towards conclusions that emphasize sophisticated condensed versions of the core argument, and a sophisticated understanding of the key debates raised by the question.
- The conclusion should take up roughly 10 per cent of an essay.
- Examples of formal essay conclusions are available in Essay 1 and Essay 2 in Section 11.

9 REFERENCING

....

- Why are references needed?
- What should be referenced?
- Basic principles
- Compiling your references

....

As you compile your own references, you may find it useful to use the list below to locate easily an appropriate example of a similar source type.

Source type	Location	Page no.
Author quoted in another text – printed	Appendix D	119
Book – electronic	Appendix D	121
Book, more than one author – printed	Section 9.3	83
Book, single author – printed	Section 9.3	81
CD-ROM	Appendix D	122
Conferencing – electronic	Appendix D	122
Edited collection – printed	Section 9.3	83
Government/official publication – electronic	Appendix D	122
Government/official publication – printed	Appendix D	120
Journal/periodical article – electronic	Appendix D	121
Journal/periodical article – printed	Section 9.3	85
Newspaper article – electronic	Appendix D	121
Newspaper article – printed	Section 9.3	85
Non-governmental organization publication – electronic	Appendix D	122
Non-governmental organization publication – printed	Appendix D	120
Personal communication	Appendix D	122
Research project – electronic	Appendix D	122

Reference writing may seem like a banal clerical activity, and it usually takes much longer than you could possibly imagine – so why do you have to do it?

9.1   Why are references needed?

There are several reasons why proper referencing is important. First, it demonstrates to those people who read your work that you are familiar with the key material on your topic and are knowledgeable about it. Second, it guards against plagiarism, since you must always acknowledge the source of any data or arguments you use that are not your own. Another reason for referencing is to allow the person who is reading your assignment to follow up any work you mention that sounds particularly interesting, or that he or she does not know. In order to do this the reader needs as much information as possible so he or she can find the work in a library, bookshop or on the internet. Accurate referencing will also help you remember particular points, or pieces of work. Finally, an essay that is properly referenced looks like a professional piece of writing, worthy of academic respect. In short:

- References guarantee the 'authority' of your argument. They allow readers to check the accuracy of the claims that your essay makes.
- References allow your readers to look up a source or argument that they want to know more about.
- References act as a reminder to the author of sources used, and make it easier for you to follow up ideas at a later stage.

9.2   What should be referenced?

The following items need to be referenced:

- Quotations.
- Diagrams, statistical information or maps reproduced or cited in your essay.
- Work that is referred to but not quoted directly (for example, if you have written 'Hall (1993) argues that . . .' or 'Research by Delamont (2000) suggests that . . .').

- Otherwise unsubstantiated arguments and assertions (for example, if you have written, 'Several commentators have argued . . .' or 'It is arguable that conventional notions of "normality" have been fundamentally challenged by the disability rights movement', you could then insert a reference or references that indicate to the reader that this idea has a considerable degree of academic respectability).

9.3   Basic principles

There are many ways to write references, but all have one feature in common: clear unambiguous details that allow someone to locate the work in a library or other source. In this section, we demonstrate the 'author/date' or 'Harvard' system for texts, commonly used in the social sciences. It is perhaps the easiest system available, and you will find it adequate for almost all purposes. (In Section 9.4 and Appendix D, you will find further guidance and examples on most of the different types of sources you are likely to need for referencing.)

Abbreviated references, including example of single author book

The Harvard system is clear and simple. Let's consider the basic principles for abbreviated references appearing in the text itself as used, say, for a book with a single author. Having written a quotation you simply add immediately after it an abbreviated reference; for example:

'In a British context, Muslims have emerged as a major target of official racial discourses and increased levels of popular violence' (Mac an Ghaill, 1999, p.76).

Note that the full stop goes outside the bracket since the abbreviated reference is all part of the sentence. If you use the author's name in your sentence, you can also write your reference like this:

> Mac an Ghaill (1999, p.76) argues that, in Britain, Muslims have increasingly become the targets of official racial discourses and racist violence.

It doesn't really matter how you lay out the abbreviated reference as long as you are consistent and as long as it contains information in the following order:

- author's name;
- date of publication (make sure this is the date of the edition in your hand);
- if applicable (e.g. if using a direct quotation or referring to a specific point), the page number(s).

If your quote is a long one then it should be indented and you can dispose of opening and closing quotation marks. Your abbreviated reference should then fall in the line immediately following the quotation. All your abbreviated references must be expanded into full references in a list at the end of your essay.

List of references, including example of single author book

At the end of the essay, in a list headed 'References', you need to write out all your references in full, organized alphabetically by authors' surnames. Let's consider first the Mac an Ghaill example above. In the reference list the entry would be:

> Mac an Ghaill, M. (1999) *Contemporary Racisms and Ethnicities: Social and Cultural Transformations*, Buckingham, Open University Press.

This entry is typical of those for a book with a single author. All similar entries in the Harvard system should:

- begin with the author's surname and initial(s);
- give the date of publication (of the *relevant* edition);
- give the title of the work;
- give details of the place of publication and the publisher.

For books you won't need to include individual page numbers because you've given these to the reader already. Your list of references will look similar to the one at the end of this book.

Basic conventions

The example we have just looked at is of a single author book, but of course you will find that material quoted or referred to can come from many different types of sources, and your reference list must reflect this. Unfortunately the basic referencing system needs a little more embellishment to cover the extra details for all but the most straight-forward references. A few more examples of sources commonly used are given below (and also in Appendix D).

First, though, let's just note two more basic conventions that it is helpful to remember:

- titles of major works, programmes, etc. (such as book and journal titles) are set in italics or underlined;
- parts of works or minor works (such as articles within journals or chapters within edited collections) are put in single quotation marks.

In addition, sometimes you will need to reference a number of works by the same author that happen to have been published in the same year. How do you differentiate them when giving an abbreviated reference? The solution is to label them '1999a', '1999b' and so on. Thus, you might write, 'Mac an Ghaill (1999a, 1999b) argues that'. When giving the full references at the end of the essay, you would then list them with the 1999a entry followed by the 1999b. (The order of 'a' and 'b' is usually determined by the order in which they occur in the essay.)

Book – more than one author

Where there are two authors, an example of the form for the abbreviated reference would be '(Epstein and Johnson, 1998)' and in the list of references:

> Epstein, D. and Johnson, R. (1998) *Schooling Sexualities*, Buckingham, Open University Press.

Where there are three or more authors, the abbreviated reference gives only the first author then 'et al.' (meaning 'and others') as in: '(Franklin et al., 2000, p.30)'. The reference list gives the names of all the authors in the order in which they appear in the work itself:

> Franklin, S., Stacey, S. and Lury, C. (2000) *Global Nature, Global Culture: Gender, Race and Life Itself*, London, Sage.

In the text itself, if you have more than one author to reference in one citation, list them alphabetically; for example '(Epstein and Johnson, 1998; Franklin et al., 2000; Mac an Ghaill, 1999)'.

Edited collection

This refers to a collection of articles or extracts compiled by one or more editors.

 If you simply refer to the book itself, treat the name(s) of the editor(s) as the author(s). The abbreviated reference,

'(Kear and Steinberg, 1999)', for example, would have this reference list entry:

Kear, A. and Steinberg, D.L. (eds) (1999) *Mourning Diana: Nation, Culture and the Performance of Grief*, London, Routledge.

If you are quoting from one of the articles/extracts in the collection, the abbreviated reference should give the name(s) of the author(s) of that article/extract and the date of the edited collection. For example, as well as being the editors of the above collection, Kear and Steinberg are also the authors of an article in it. The abbreviated reference for this article should thus read '(Kear and Steinberg, 1999)', while the full reference will have both the names of the author(s) and the editor(s):

Kear A. and Steinberg, D.L. (1999) 'Ghost writing' in Kear, A. and Steinberg, D.L. (eds) *Mourning Diana: Nation, Culture and the Performance of Grief*, London, Routledge.

This is unproblematic unless, in the course of your essay, you cite both the article, 'Ghost writing', and the book, *Mourning Diana*, as separate entries. For example, you might refer to the book in one paragraph and the specific article two paragraphs down. In such circumstances you would have to follow the advice above for citing works by the same author published in the same year. Thus you might identify the book as '(Kear and Steinberg, 1999a)' and the article as '(Kear and Steinberg, 1999b)'.

Some formats require that, in a full reference, you state the page numbers of articles/extracts in edited collections in the same manner as articles in journals (see below). However, this practice is not uniform.

Journal/periodical article

If the article you are referring to or quoting from appears in a journal or other periodical, the abbreviated reference takes the usual format: '(Westwood, 2000, p.188)'. In the full reference you include details of the journal volume/number and the page numbers between which the article appears, but you don't include place of publication or publisher's name. For example:

Westwood, S. (2000) 'Re-branding Britain: sociology, futures and futurology', *Sociology*, vol.34, no.1, pp.185–202.

Newspaper article

These follow much the same pattern as journal articles, although omitting in the full reference the page numbers between which the item appears. An abbreviated reference would be '(Mansfield, 2000, p.21)' and its full reference would have the date of publication at the end:

Mansfield, M. (2000) 'White on black', *The Guardian*, 17 February.

Other media and conventions

Electronic sources are increasingly being used, both online and CD-ROM. The basic principles still largely apply but for online sources, because of the transitory nature of the material, you need to include the date on which it was accessed. Further details and examples are given in Appendix D.

Appendix E lists some abbreviations and foreign words in common use, including some frequently found in references. You are not expected to use all these conventions, but as your essay writing skills develop you may find some are quicker to use. If you do use them you must do so correctly.

You will see authors using a range of different formats from the Harvard system, such as '(Mac an Ghaill, 1999: 76)' (for the abbreviated reference in the text). You will also find authors using a footnote numbering system for the abbreviated reference, with the full reference at the bottom of the page or at the end of the text. Whatever the system, the general rules for what information is required are the same, only the positioning is different.

9.4 Compiling your references

It's a good idea to familiarize yourself with the basic principles for writing references as set out above before you begin to access your sources. Then, *at the time* you are researching your sources, keep to hand this section and Appendix D in which we have listed further examples of the reference types you are most likely to need. Note down all the details you will require (you don't need to worry about getting the format exactly right at this point). Almost all of us have at some time omitted to do this and learned how difficult it is to trace the reference details afterwards – usually at the very moment that the essay is ready to hand in.

Perhaps the best advice here is to try to remember the basic format and then look up the further details as you need them. Certainly you should not be intimidated by what looks like a complex process. Get started on the basics using the guidance above and then simply refer to the specific examples as you need them.

....

Summary

• To write a reference using the Harvard system you should give an abbreviated reference in the text and full details in a list of references at the end of the text.

- Abbreviated references in the text are written: author's surname, publication date, and page number(s) if applicable.
- Full references at the end of the text are listed alphabetically by author/originator.
- References for different publications by the same author in the same year are distinguished using the 'a', 'b', etc. convention.
- Full references at the end of the text for a single author book are written: author's surname and initials, publication date, title (italicized or underlined), place of publication and publisher. Electronic references follow similar principles as those for printed texts but must also include the date of access.
- References to chapters in edited collections, to journal and newspaper articles, and to various other sources are given in slightly different ways. Details of these are in this section and Appendix D.
- Appendix E includes some abbreviations that are sometimes used when referencing, particularly when using the alternative footnote numbering system.
- Note down your reference details at the time you are finding your material.
- Referencing is a basic academic skill and it is almost certain that you will be expected to use references accurately on undergraduate courses.

....

10 SOME COMMON WORRIES

....

- Plagiarism
- Writing too much
- Using the 'I' word
- Using your own experience
- Presentation, spelling and grammar

....

It is difficult to identify or predict all the worries that you may have in writing essays. But there are a few important points to know about and some things to avoid, so read this section carefully.

10.1 Plagiarism

Plagiarism means using someone else's work and passing it off as your own. It refers to copying other people's work word for word, or making only minor changes to it with the intention of representing it as your own. This does not mean that you are forbidden to use every word or phrase that appears in a text from which you are working. In particular, you will almost certainly need to repeat technical vocabulary. For example, it would look rather odd if an essay on Marxist theory avoided key conceptual categories such as 'class struggle' or 'relation to the means of production'. The problem occurs when you recycle whole sentences or paragraphs without indicating that these are quotations or paraphrased from your original source.

   Of course, the question is how to avoid plagiarizing in the first place. A lot of people plagiarize unintentionally. Here are a few reasons why it may occur:

- *Bad note taking*
  Sometimes you may find yourself copying chunks of text into your notes and then failing to put these in quotation marks. Similarly, when taking notes you may sometimes paraphrase from a source without putting the argument in your own words. In each case, these may then appear in your essay as an argument that bears a remarkable similarity to your source material.

- *Lack of confidence*
  If an argument is very complex or you are particularly unclear about it, you may stick to your original source as closely as possible so you don't 'get it wrong' or because of a feeling that the words could not be improved upon. The problem is that the person who marks your essay won't be able to tell whether you have understood the argument or not since you won't have reproduced it in your own terms.

To avoid plagiarism, adopt good note-taking habits, always ask for help if you don't understand something, and re-read your essays before submitting them. Tutors can usually spot plagiarism because the style or tone of the writing will suddenly change. If you reread your essays you too will be able to notice when this happens.

It is important to get on top of this issue for a number of reasons. Most obviously, plagiarized work is likely to attract a fail grade. However, plagiarizing work is also of little educational benefit to you. The process of putting arguments into your own words is a crucial part of grasping ideas and committing them to memory. It also helps you to learn how to use and apply the ideas *for yourself.* Plagiarism, if nothing else, is thus a waste of your time since it probably means that you have not thoroughly understood what you have written.

Occasionally some people will deliberately plagiarize in an essay. This is a serious offence, since it is a form of academic theft. In the case of assessed course work, it is also an attempt to gain qualifications by cheating. Deliberate plagiarism may incur such penalties as your institution determines.

> ### Advice for OU students
>
> If you are tempted to plagiarize because you are having problems with the course or have fallen behind with your work, telephone your OU tutor or seek OU counselling help instead. Your tutor or counselling service will help you identify a much better solution to the problem. General advice about avoiding plagiarism should be sought from your tutor in the first instance. The University's regulations on plagiarism are set out in the *Student Handbook*.

10.2   Writing too much

Most essays have word limits. Many students point out that they could easily write a whole lot more on any one topic. Indeed, people write 80,000-word books on the sort of issues that you address in your essays, so everyone knows that word limits can be rather restrictive. However, they are not set merely to irritate you. Shorter essays are an important academic tool. In writing them, you learn how to prioritize and select material, and how to condense big topics into a punchy, easily digested form. These are academic skills that you will need even in writing much longer pieces. We know that it is painful but, if you're writing too much, be ruthless. Concentrate on the biggest, most important arguments and examples and cut the rest. Your work will almost certainly be better for it.

You need to remember that on some courses marks may be deducted for an over-long essay (always check the regulations covering the specific course that you are studying). Furthermore, some markers may feel that writing over length allows you to cover a topic in more detail than other people and thus confers an unfair advantage on you.

10.3 Using the 'I' word

Sometimes you will be told that the first person pronoun ('I') should be avoided in social science essays (for example, that you should not write 'In this essay I intend to explore . . .'). This is because 'I' is sometimes thought to indicate a lack of objectivity. In this case, you can often ignore personal pronouns completely (for example, by writing 'This essay will explore . . .'). In fact, there are no hard and fast rules about using 'I' in social science essays. Different disciplines (and different individuals) tend to adopt different conventions. Clearly, in your writing you will want to avoid the excessive repetition of any word or phrase and 'I' is no exception. Perhaps the best way to find out whether the use of 'I' is appropriate to the particular course you are studying is to check with the person marking your work.

10.4 Using your own experience

Some essay questions will explicitly ask you to draw on your own personal experience – indeed, autobiography is a recognized research method in the social sciences. Additionally, relevant personal experience is sometimes used to add 'colour' to an argument or to grab the reader's attention.

Having said this, there can be a danger that, in the context of social scientific writing, personal experience will sound like 'bar-room philosophy'. In other words, it will be little more than unsubstantiated personal opinion. If you use personal experience you will need to demonstrate clearly how and why it is relevant to both the question and the course, and be able to substantiate any claims that you make on the basis of it.

10.5 Presentation, spelling and grammar

Your essays will be marked first and foremost on their content. However, spelling, grammar and punctuation are important in essay writing. The baseline here is that essays should be readable and make sense. Your spelling, grammar and punctuation need to be good enough to communicate effectively to your reader and, at degree level or equivalent, this implies the ability to use conventions of spelling, grammar and punctuation correctly (see, for example, The Open University, 1998).

As a result, you should choose your words appropriately and correctly. Use of 'jargon' words has already been mentioned in 'Clear sentences and paragraphs' (in Section 7.4). If you use abbreviations or foreign words make sure you use them correctly (Appendix E has a list of those commonly found).

For further advice on use of written English see the resources listed in Appendix F.

Advice for OU students

If you have any concerns about any of the above or similar matters, particularly if you want support in developing your written English, you should consult your tutor or seek advice from OU counselling services.

For guidance on submitting tutor marked assignments consult your course assignment booklet. The regulations governing essay extensions are set out in the *Student Handbook*.

Summary

- Plagiarism means copying someone else's work and claiming it as your own. Plagiarized essays will normally attract a fail grade. Deliberate plagiarism, which constitutes cheating, may result in disciplinary action.
- Plagiarism is often unintentional. To avoid this make sure that you write essay notes in your own words and always put quotations in quotation marks or indent the

text; reread your essays, looking for sudden changes in style or tone; and seek help if you do not understand particular points to ensure that, when writing, you can reproduce them in your own words.

- Writing to a word limit is an important academic skill: it teaches you to condense complex material into its component parts, and to select and communicate core arguments.
- Personal experience can be a useful source of evidence and some courses require you to use it. However, be careful to relate it to the course and the essay question and to substantiate your claims.
- Essays are expected to be readable and to use conventions of spelling, grammar and punctuation correctly.

11 EXAMPLES OF STUDENT ESSAYS

....

If you haven't already done so, read through the following examples of student essays. Essay 1 illustrates how applying the basic standards we have been discussing really can help to produce a good essay. It is a strong essay displaying more advanced writing skills. Depending on the exact requirements of the course, it would probably receive a grade at the top of the range. In contrast, Essay 2 is a weaker essay suggesting less developed social scientific writing skills. Although it might gain a pass mark, it would probably be towards the bottom of the grade range. The word limit for each is 2000 words.

Essay 1

'School is a significant site in which sex/gender is produced'. Discuss.

This essay critically explores the claim that school is a significant site in which sex/gender is produced. The claim derives from a broadly social constructionist position, namely one that views sex/gender as being the product of social meanings and practices rather than something biologically given. The essay begins by outlining the social constructionist critique of the biological account of sex/gender. It then reviews recent research on gender and schooling to explore the extent to which the social meanings and practices that make up life in school may be seen as producing relational forms of masculinity and femininity. In exploring these issues, the essay endorses a broadly social constructionist standpoint on gender and schooling, although it also seeks to highlight a number of potential limitations to this position, particularly as these relate to the literature's account of the body and social agency.

Conventional or 'common sense' accounts tend to view masculinity and femininity as biological categories characterized by a range of fixed physical and psychological differences in which the supposed attributes of masculinity (for example, rationality and the capacity for physical action) are valued over those of femininity (for example, intuition and the capacity for caring). The feminist cultural theorist Chris Weedon (1999) locates the origins of these ideas (at least in their contemporary form) in nineteenth century biological theory and in Victorian middle-class values. However, she also points out that they have been reinvigorated in more recent work in the fields of sociobiology and evolutionary psychology (see, for example: Thornhill and Palmer, 2000; Wilson, 1978).

The social constructionist position takes issue with this biologically reductive account. Drawing, in particular, on the work of Michel Foucault (1977, 1984) commentators from this perspective have sought to argue that masculinity and femininity cannot be understood as fixed biological categories but are instead produced in and through social meanings and practices. This position is distinct from earlier sociological accounts of 'sex role' (see, for example, Rossi, 1985). Earlier accounts had tended to view gender as the social elaboration of an underlying biological sex difference. Social constructionist theory, on the other hand, argues that the notion of biological sex difference is itself a social construct. For example, Thomas Lacquer (1990) has demonstrated that the notion of distinct male and female bodies arose in the nineteenth century. Prior to this maleness and femaleness were seen as variations on a single body. Equally, Judith Butler (1993) has argued that sex/gender is a 'performative enactment'. She suggests that – like other categories of the person – maleness and femaleness do not precede social meanings and practices but are brought into existence through an active 'gendering', that is the citation of sex/ gender 'norms' embodied in what, following Foucault, she refers to as discursive practices. Importantly, Butler (1993, p.238) also argues that gender is systematically (though not inevitably) produced through a 'heterosexual matrix' which equates 'proper' forms of masculinity and femininity with heterosexuality and identifies gay masculinities and lesbian femininities as, in some way, 'failed' or 'damaged'.

*Bob Connell's influential work in the sociology of masculinity
endorses this critique of biological essentialism but questions
whether it risks writing the body out of existence. Connell
suggests that forms of masculinity and femininity cannot be
reduced to supposed biological differences but argues that bodies
have 'forms of recalcitrance to social symbolism and control' (see,
in particular, Connell, 1995, p.56).*

*Connell also suggests that Butler's 'hard' social constructionist
account risks writing social agency out of existence. Connell
argues that there are multiple versions of masculinity (and, by
implication, femininity) that are actively produced through
relations of similarity to and difference from key social others.
For example, forms of 'laddish', heterosexual white working-class
masculinity may be defined in opposition to forms of 'respectable'
middle-class masculinity, to non-white ethnicities, to forms of
femininity and to gay masculinities. This argument places a
greater emphasis than does Butler's on the notion of pupils as
'active makers of their own sex/gender identities' (Mac an Ghaill,
1994, p.90). Thus, whereas Butler tends to downplay agency (the
active 'speaking' of sex/gender) in favour of a notion of
performativity (being 'spoken by' social meanings and practices),
Connell retains a stronger account of it.*

*Drawing on the work of the Italian Marxist Antonio Gramsci
(1971), Connell also argues that masculinities and femininities
can be understood as being engaged in 'hegemonic struggle'. This
refers to an ongoing and potentially shifting process of
competition, negotiation, alliance-building and sometimes
coercion whereby, under particular conditions, particular
versions of masculinity and femininity come to be 'culturally
exalted' or 'idealized' while other versions are marginalized and
subordinated (see, Connell, 1990, p.83).*

*Broadly social constructionist ideas of this kind have informed a
body of recent literature on sex/gender and schooling (see, for
example, Epstein and Johnson, 1998; Kehily and Nayak, 1996;
Mac an Ghaill, 1994; Martino, 1999; Thorne, 1993; Sewell, 1997;
Wolpe, 1988). Within this literature, schools are seen as
significant sites in which sex/gender is actively produced. This is
to say that sex/gender is viewed not as something that is simply*

brought into the school ready formed but as something actively produced and reproduced in the processes and practices of schooling itself. This active production of sex/gender has a number of dimensions and the following discussion focuses on three of these: the ways in which the content and practices of schooling encode sex/gender; the ways in which pupils actively use sex/gender to negotiate schooling; and the ways in which sex/gender intersects with other social relations.

Perhaps the most obvious means by which sex/gender is said to be produced in the social constructionist literature is via the content and practices of schooling itself. For example, Thorne's (1993) study of two US elementary schools draws attention to the ways in which the categorization of children by gender is threaded through the material and social fabric of the school, such as in teachers' talk ('There's three girls need to get busy', p. 34) or the organization and management of learning (for instance, dividing pupils into gender-based 'teams', p. 67). Similarly, Epstein and Johnson (1994, p.214) point to the ways in which the regulation of pupils' clothing (in particular, sanctions against girls' clothing thought to connote too overt a sexuality) frequently embodies notions of 'appropriate' or 'proper' forms of gender. While Thorne (1993, pp.35-36) draws attention to the fact that many aspects of schooling will also play down or contradict gender categorizations, it remains the case that the content and practices of schooling encode sex/gender as a significant category of difference.

However, while sex/gender can be said to be encoded in the content and practices of schooling, the literature also suggests that pupils are themselves active agents in its production. Thorne (1993), for example, describes the children in her study as engaging in 'borderwork', practices by which they actively produce, strengthen and assert sex/gender differences. For instance, she describes a game of team hand-ball which began as a co-operative and informal activity in which gender was not strongly marked but which rapidly accelerated into a more aggressive interaction themed as 'the boys against the girls' (p.65). In this moment, Thorne suggests, sex/gender was being actively produced (or in Butler's terms, 'performatively enacted') as a significant category of difference.

As well as producing sex/gender through friendship group interactions, the literature also suggests that pupils use sex/ gender to negotiate and resist schooling. Kehily and Nayak (1996, p.214) describe an account from a group of secondary school pupils in which one of them (Samantha) was claimed to have pursued a teacher (Mr. Smedley) round the classroom with a sprig of mistletoe with the intention of 'getting some lipstick on the top of his head'. In this instance, a heterosexualized form of femininity is used satirically to undermine the authority of a male teacher (see also Walkerdine, 1981).

While heterosexualized forms of sex/gender are clearly deployed to subvert adult authority, it is also possible to argue that sex/ gender is used to negotiate schooling in more subtle ways. For instance, Connell has argued that boys use masculinity to negotiate or build a 'subjective orientation' to the curriculum and that, in the process, the curriculum is important in producing differentiated forms of masculinity. He writes:

> *the differentiation of masculinities occurs in relation to a school curriculum that organizes knowledge hierarchically, and sorts students into an academic hierarchy. By institutionalizing academic failure via competitive grading and streaming, the school forces differentiation on the boys. . . . Social power in terms of access to higher education, entry to professions, command of communication, is being delivered by the school system to boys who are academic 'successes'. The reaction of the 'failed' is likely to be a claim to other sources of power, even other definitions of masculinity. Sporting prowess, physical aggression, sexual conquest, may do.*
> *(Connell, 1993, p.95)*

This general argument informs Máirtín Mac an Ghaill's (1994) study of a multi-ethnic English secondary school. Mac an Ghaill identifies a variety of differentiated masculinities – the 'macho lads', the 'academic achievers', the 'new enterprisers', and the 'real Englishmen' – through which boys in the school collectively negotiated the curriculum, their home backgrounds and their perceived employment futures. The 'new enterprisers' were, perhaps, particularly interesting in that they broke with the conventional distinction (identified by Connell, above) between anti-academic, 'laddish' forms of masculinity, and pro-school masculinities validated by academic success. Mac an Ghaill argues that the 'new enterprisers' were able to build a pro-school masculine identification out of a newly vocationalized curriculum that offered recognition for academic success in non-traditional subject areas, especially Information and Communication Technologies.

The final area highlighted by the social constructionist literature as a means by which sex/gender is produced in the school concerns the ways in which masculinities and femininities are produced in and through relations of similarity to and difference from social others. As discussed above, Thorne's (1993) concept of 'borderwork' draws our attention to the ways in which sex/ gender is used by pupils to produce themselves in gender-differentiated terms. This opposition between forms of masculinity and femininity is perhaps the most central relation underpinning pupils' sex/gender identifications in the school. However, both Mac an Ghaill (1994) and Epstein and Johnson (1998) underline the extent to which school-based masculinities and femininities are also produced in and through relations of age, class, ethnicity and sexuality, as well as in relation to forms of masculinity and femininity deemed subordinate or otherwise inferior.

For instance, Epstein and Johnson cite an exchange between a group of four Muslim girls in a large single-sex comprehensive in which a fifth girl is described in the following terms:

> *Shamira is not traditional [i.e. she does not occupy a conservative form of Muslim ethnicity]. She is a big tart and wears lipstick that doesn't suit her and she walks around sticking her tits out.*
> *Epstein and Johnson (1998, p.117)*

The girls in this example can be seen to be constructing their own femininity in opposition to Shamira whose femininity is deemed inappropriately westernized and sexualized. This, then, is an example where sex/gender is spoken through intra-ethnic identifications (traditional versus westernized) and through an opposition to a subordinated femininity (the 'madonna' versus the 'whore'). As Epstein and Johnson also argue, although drawing on wider social relations, such gender constructions occur within and are specific to the dynamics of individual schools.

The girls' appraisal of Shamira in terms of sexuality underlines the centrality of sex and sexuality to the production and policing of gender in pupils' cultures. Mac an Ghaill (1994, pp.90–96), for instance, describes the ways in which the secondary school boys in his study worked at producing masculinity through 'competitive and compulsive' sexualized talk and practice within their friendship groups. This consisted of the sexual-objectification of girls and women and the homophobic harassment of boys perceived as gay or 'insufficiently masculine'. Epstein and Johnson (1998, p.158) suggest that anti-lesbian harassment appears less central to girls' culture than does anti-gay harassment to boys' culture. Nevertheless, as the Shamira example demonstrates, they argue that heterosexualized appraisal of other girls is central to the production of femininity within girls' friendship groups.

The recent social constructionist literature has, therefore, made a systematic case in support of the proposition that schooling is a significant site in which sex/gender is produced. It argues that the content and practices of schooling encode sex/gender; that pupils actively use gender to negotiate schooling; and that gender is produced within local pupils' cultures through relations of similarity to and difference from key social others. Work on the relationship between gender and sexuality in the context of the school has been particularly significant. Such arguments, I would argue, fundamentally undermine biologically determinist readings of sex/gender. Nevertheless, it may be possible to qualify the social constructionist account. In particular, following Connell, it is possible to argue that the theoretical tension between a 'hard' social constructionist account (in which social agency is replaced by a notion of performativity) and the emphasis in the literature on pupils as 'active makers of sex/ gender identities' is not fully addressed or resolved. Equally, it may also be possible to argue that the literature does not fully resolve the exact status of the body in the social constructionist account. However, it remains the case that the recent literature on gender and schooling significantly adds to our understanding of the social construction of gender and sexuality.

References

Butler, J. (1993) *Bodies That Matter*, London, Routledge.

Connell, R.W. (1990) 'An iron man: the body and some contradictions of hegemonic masculinity' in Messner, M.A. and Sabo, D.F. (eds) *Sport, Men and the Gender Order: Critical Feminist Perspectives*, Champaign, IL, Human Kinetics.

Connell, R.W. (1993) 'Cool guys, swots and wimps: the interplay of masculinity and education', in Angus, L. (ed.) *Education, Inequality and Social Identity*, London, Falmer Press.

Connell, R.W. (1995) *Masculinities*, Cambridge, Polity Press.

Epstein, D. and Johnson, R. (1994) 'On the straight and the narrow: the heterosexual presumption, homophobias and schools' in Epstein, D. (ed.) *Challenging Lesbian and Gay Inequalities in Education*, Buckingham, Open University Press.

Epstein, D. and Johnson, R. (1998) *Schooling Sexualities*, Buckingham, Open University Press.

Foucault, M. (1977) *Discipline and Punish: The Birth of the Prison*, Harmondsworth, Penguin.

Foucault, M. (1984) *The History of Sexuality, Vol. 1: An Introduction*, Harmondsworth, Penguin/Peregrine.

Gramsci, A. (1971) *Selections from Prison Notebooks*, London, Lawrence and Wishart.

Kehily, M.J. and Nayak, A. (1996) 'The Christmas kiss: sexuality, storytelling and schooling', *Curriculum Studies*, 4(2), pp.211–228.

Lacquer, T.W. (1990) *Making Sex: Body and Gender from the Greeks to Freud*, Cambridge, MA, Harvard University Press.

Mac an Ghaill, M. (1994) *The Making of Men: Masculinities, Sexualities and Schooling*, Buckingham, Open University Press.

Martino, W. (1999) 'Cool boys, party animals, squids and poofters: interrogating the dynamics and politics of adolescent masculinities in school', *British Journal of Sociology of Education*, vol.20, pp.239–263.

Rossi, A.S. (1985) 'Gender and parenthood' in Rossi, A.S. (ed.) *Gender and the Life Course*, New York, Aldine.

Sewell, T. (1997) *Black Masculinities and Schooling: How Black Boys Survive Modern Schooling*, Stoke-on-Trent, Trentham.

Thorne, B. (1993) *Gender Play: Girls and Boys in School*, Buckingham, Open University Press.

Thornhill, R. and Palmer, C.T. (2000) *A Natural History of Rape: Biological Bases of Sexual Coercion*, Cambridge, Mass., MIT Press.

Walkerdine, V. (1981) 'Sex, power and pedagogy', *Screen Education*, no.38, pp.14–24.

Weedon, C. (1999) *Feminism, Theory and the Politics of Difference*, Oxford, Blackwell.

Wilson, E.O. (1978) *On Human Nature*, Cambridge, MA, Harvard University Press.

Wolpe, A-M. (1988) *Within School Walls: The Role of Discipline, Sexuality and the Curriculum*, London, Routledge.

Commentary on Essay 1

In reviewing this essay we are not particularly concerned as to whether the answer is 'right' or not. The literature it draws on is from cultural studies and sociology and it is undoubtedly the case that the question of sex/gender could have been addressed from a number of alternative disciplinary points of view – for example, developmental psychology or biology – that might have generated different arguments. Instead, the issue of interest to us is the extent to which the answer demonstrates effective social scientific writing skills.

As with any piece of work, the essay is not without flaws. For instance, it could be argued that evidence in support of the 'conventional' view of gender is not explored systematically enough to be rejected with such certainty by the author (although this may simply reflect the balance of argument in the literature the author was required to read). Equally, it could be argued that the concept of sex/gender 'performativity' is not fully explained and that it is not fully illustrated through the research evidence cited. Similarly, the critique of the literature on schooling and sex/gender in the conclusion (the arguments about the status of the body and social agency) appear to repeat Connell's theoretical points without really growing out of the evidence explored in the main section of the essay.

Having said this, the essay has a number of strengths that suggest it should receive a grade towards the top end of the range. Let's explore these in terms of structure and writing skills, content and social scientific skills.

Structure and writing skills

- The essay begins with an introduction that identifies the subject of the essay, indicates the debate lying 'behind' the question, signposts its content and establishes the author's position. (See Section 6.1.)
- The main section uses a standard 'evaluative' structure, that is, it outlines competing positions then explores the evidence for and against them before coming to a conclusion. (See Section 4.2.)
- It builds a logically progressing argument that develops through the following steps: the social constructionist argument is more convincing than the conventional biological account; this is because sex/gender is 'performative' and relational; this can be demonstrated in relation to schooling. (See Section 7.1.)
- It 'flows' reasonably smoothly, is well signposted throughout (see paragraphs 1 and 7), makes use of summary/introductory points (for example, in the statement, 'As well as producing sex/gender through friendship group interactions, the literature also suggests that . . .') and makes accurate use of spelling, grammar, paragraphing and sentence structure. (See Section 7.4.)
- It provides an evaluative conclusion that summarizes the preceding argument, provides a clear endorsement of the statement in the question, and identifies potential absences in the argument. (See Section 8.)
- It is slightly long (2,200 words) but is probably just on the outer limits of acceptability. (As with other regulations, remember to check the rules on essay length that apply to the actual course you are studying.)

Content

Effective coverage of theoretical issues and research evidence is clearly central to any essay answer. The author of this essay appears to have used or referenced a range of relevant sources and provided detailed coverage of both theoretical material and research evidence. Without knowing the exact content of the course she or he was studying it is difficult to comment on this in much detail but the coverage looks thorough and the detailed handling of the material suggests wide-ranging reading and a good understanding of the issues.

Social scientific skills

- The answer addresses the question set. (See Sections 5.2 and 6.1.)
- The essay is effectively referenced, including page details where necessary. (See Section 9.)
- It makes good use of relevant quotations. The Connell quotation is a 'classic' statement of the social constructionist position. The quotation from Epstein and Johnson adds some 'colour' to the argument and is effective in illustrating and illuminating a complex argument. Both support rather than replace points made by the author. (See Section 7.3.)
- Within the confines of a 2000-word essay, it provides a complex and thorough engagement with relevant theory and applies this theory to and supports it with empirical evidence. (See Sections 3.2 and 7.2.)
- The essay demonstrates effective skills of selection and summary. (See Section 7.2.)
- It provides an effective evaluation of relevant concepts, debates and evidence. (See Sections 4.2 and 7.2.)
- It comes to a clear conclusion that is supported by the preceding argument. (See Section 8.)
- It makes good use of appropriate academic vocabulary and concepts. (See Sections 7.2 and 7.4.)

Now let's take a look at Essay 2, the weaker of the two essays.

Essay 2

'School is a significant site in which sex/gender is produced'. Discuss.

This essay looks at the arguments for and against the idea that school is a significant site in which gender is produced. The first section shows where this idea comes from and contrasts it to the deterministic account. The second section gives evidence in favour of the theory of Social Constructionism.

We are used to thinking that gender is biological. Men are men and women are women and this is natural. Sociobiologists and evolutionary psychologists would agree with this point of view. This is called 'Deterministic'. Men are better at rational tasks and thinking in three dimensions. They are also stronger. Women are better at intuition thinking and emotionality. E.O.Wilson is an example of this approach.

However, writers such as Foucolt, Butler and Connell have challenged this. They argue that gender is constructed in practices and meanings, such as the 'enactment of gender norms'. Butler calls this 'performativity'.

Connell argues that gender is 'hegemonic'. This means that there are different types of masculinity in competition but that certain types (such as sportsmen) are 'idealized' (Connell, 1990). Connell got this idea from Gramsci, an Italian Marxist. An example of hegemonic masculinity is given by Swain who argues that playing football in the playground makes boys dominant in the school because this draws on a sporting version of masculinity that is dominant in the wider society (Swain, 2000).

Foucolt is very important in this Social Constructionist theory. He argued that the term 'homosexual' does not refer to a pre-existing identity but constructs that identity. This does not mean that same-sex sexual activity did not happen before the nineteenth century (when the term homosexual was invented), it means that that same-sex sexual activity did not imply a particular type of personality (the homosexual) before this. The homosexual is therefore Socially Constructed as of course is the heterosexual. Butler argues that biological sex is also a Social Construction (Butler, 1993).

Schools are a place where Social Construction happens. This has been argued by many eminent Academic thinkers including Mac an Ghaill and Epstein. Connell argues that masculinities appear in relation to the curriculum.

> *the differentiation of masculinities occurs in relation to a school curriculum that organizes knowledge hierarchically, and sorts students into an academic hierarchy. By institutionalizing academic failure via competitive grading and streaming, the school forces differentiation on the boys. . . . Social power in terms of access to higher education, entry to professions, command of communication, is being delivered by the school system to boys who are academic 'successes'. The reaction of the 'failed' is likely to be a claim to other sources of power, even other definitions of masculinity. Sporting prowess, physical aggression, sexual conquest, may do. (Connell, 1993)*

This is one way that schools Socially Construct gender.

A second way is that children actively produce gender for themselves. Take the example of children lining up to leave the classroom. They used to be told to form lines so that girls were in one line and boys were in another. In fact, I remember that in my first school it still had two entrances one marked for boys and the other for girls. Foucolt would see this as an example of the ways in which schools produce sexual difference. Now however girls and boys will be told to form a single line but Barry Thorne argues they will still try to form lines according to gender.

This is an example of boys and girls actively producing gender for themselves which Thorn calls 'borderwork' (Thorn, 1993).

Sexuality is a big theme in much of this writing on schooling and gender. There are lots of examples where children use sexuality to try to undermine there teachers. A famous one is Valerie Walkerdines example of two little boys calling their nursery teacher rude names. Many people are surprised that children as young as this would dare to be so cheeky. Another example is the 'Christmas kiss' story told by Kehily and Nayak (1996). In this case a secondary school girl chased her male teacher round the classroom with a sprig of mistletoe and claimed she was trying to kiss him on the head. The pupils liked to retell this story so that the story itself was one way in which they 'had a laff' and resisted the authority of the school. Unfortunately the teacher had a nervous breakdown. These examples also show how gender is used in the classroom to 'negotiate the curriculum' indicating how schools Socially Construct gender.

Mac an Ghaill (1994) is very interested in the ways in which boys use homophobic abuse to police other boys. To be identified as a sissy is to invite homophobic abuse whether or not on defines oneself as gay, often in the form of more or less ritualized humour. The use of humour and insult constitutes a regulatory practice by young men in schools through which they establish and exhibit heterosexual masculinities. The forms humour and insult employed are primarily either sexist (for example, the teasing and harassment of girls or insult to other boys via insulting their mothers or sisters) or homophobic abuse of young men who did not display 'hyper-masculinity'. Swain talks about this too. He describes how the football-playing boys in his research would abuse boys who weren't very good at football by calling them 'Gaylord' and 'poofter'. Since these boys were at primary school calling them homosexual was not because they were homosexual but because this was a way of saying they were like girls. The point Swain is making is that football is a dominant form of masculinity in our society and that the boys in the school tried to lay claim to dominance in there own right by being good at football. However, this dominance was also at the expense of other social groups such as girls, homosexuals and boys who weren't any good at football. Mac an Ghaill argues that boys 'make up' collective identities as boys out of a Compulsory Heterosexuality, Misogyny and Homophobia.

> *heterosexual male students were involved in a double relationship, of traducing the 'other', including women and gays (external relations), at the same time as expelling femininity and homosexuality from within themselves (internal relations).*

> *(Man an Ghaill, p.90)*

Barry Thorne describes how one boy in her research was called a 'sissy' by other boys because he wore a one-piece snow suit which they thought was 'wimpy' and because he liked to play girl's games in the playground as well as playing boys games. She says he was a bit of a loner and didn't have many friends. Some children were more likely to get away with this sort of thing. A girl got away with it because she was a good athlete and because she could fight which gave her respect with the other children. But one of the teachers described her as 'wanting to be a boy'.

There are three ways that schools produce gender. The pupils produce gender for themselves. The school produces gender through things like making children line up in different lines. And the children 'negotiate the curriculum'.

In conclusion, this has essay has presented a lot of evidence to show that 'school is a significant site in which gender is produced'. In fact, Christine Heward describes schools as 'masculinity factories' and I would tend to agree with her. Gender is obviously very important in the school day. Schools are always doing things that reproduce gender even though they sometimes try to do the opposite of this. And even when schools do try do the opposite of this the children themselves resist this by reproducing conventional ideas about gender (Thorne). Butler calls this 'Performativity' but you could see it from the 'Deterministic' point of view of which EO Wilson is an example which would argue that the children are just being boys and girls because they are programmed to be this way by Evolution. This argument is difficult to get away from at the end of the day because there are some obvious differences between men and women so we probably should expect to see these in children as well. I would argue that we need to have a Middle Ground where we put together the Deterministic and the Social Constructionist point of views. In fact, this is what Connell argues when he says that you cant get away from the body.

The body, I would conclude is inescapable (Connell)

This is what I would argue.

References

Butler, J. (1993) 'Bodies That Matter'.
Connell, R.W. (1995) *Masculinities*, Polity Press.
Epstein, D. and Johnson, R. (1998) *Schooling Sexualities*, Buckingham: Open University Press.

Foucault, (1977) *Discipline and Punish: The Birth of the Prison*,
Kehily, M.J. and Nayak, A. (1996) 'The Christmas kiss: Sexuality, storytelling and schooling', Curriculum Studies
Mac an Ghaill, M. (1994) 'The Making of Men: Masculinities, Sexualities and Schooling', Buckingham: Open University Press.
Swain, J. (2000) 'The money's good, the fame's good, the girls are good: the role of playground football in the construction of young boys' masculinity in a junior school', *British Journal of Sociology of Education*, 21, 1: 95–109.

Commentary on Essay 2

You can probably see for yourself that this essay is not as strong an answer to the question as that provided by Essay 1. Why is this? Again, we can break down our thoughts into issues related to structure and writing skills, content and social scientific skills.

Structure and writing skills

Although the essay has an introduction, conclusion and limited signposting, its structure and the writing skills displayed are weak. In particular:

- The introduction is underdeveloped compared to Essay 1. It does not establish the author's position on the question and both the signposting and the allusion to the debate lying 'behind' the question are vague. (See Section 6.1.)
- There are systematic errors in spelling and punctuation (e.g. 'there' instead of 'their'; incorrect use of the apostrophe; unnecessary use of capital letters on terms such as 'social constructionism'), sentences are sometimes cumbersome and paragraphs are sometimes too short. (See Section 10.5.)
- There are errors in the spelling of several authors' names (Foucolt instead of Foucault; Barry Thorne instead of Barrie Thorne).

- The brief section beginning, 'To be identified as a sissy is to invite homophobic abuse . . .', and ending, 'homophobic abuse of young men who did not display 'hypermasculinity', is plagiarized from Epstein and Johnson (1998, p.181). (See Section 10.1.)
- Although the essay begins by discussing theory and then moves on to look at empirical evidence, the logical progression of the argument is problematic. For instance, the relevance of paragraph 5 to the question needs to be more clearly established while the material on sexuality and schooling is not clearly located as an example of the ways in which gender is produced in schooling practices. (See Section 7.1.)
- Given the word limit, the essay is probably slightly short (1,500 words). (Remember to check the rules on essay length that apply to the actual course you are studying.)

Content

The material covered appears to be relevant to the question set, drawing on similar literature to Essay 1. However, the understanding of this material appears to be much shallower in comparison to Essay 1 and the breadth of detailed reading (as evidenced in the identification of major arguments and relevant evidence) appears more limited.

Social scientific skills

Once again, these areas are weak compared to Essay 1.

- Referencing is inconsistent and incomplete. (See Section 9.)
- The introduction and conclusion are thin. (See Sections 6 and 8.)

- Handling of theory is poor, suggesting an inadequate understanding of the material. For example, although the discussion of Foucault and homosexuality is good, the concepts of performativity and hegemony are not fully explained. (See Sections 3.2 and 7.2.)
- Both the Mac an Ghaill quotation and the first Connell quotation are used without a full explanation of the points being made. (See Section 7.3.)
- The empirical evidence is sometimes left to 'speak for itself' without a full explanation of the point it is being used to illustrate or support. (See Section 7.2.)
- The information cited about the author's own school-days detracts from the professionalism of the argument by appearing merely anecdotal. (See Section 10.4.)
- The evaluative conclusion is undermined by an incorrect understanding of Connell's argument about the relationship between the body and the social.
- Use of appropriate academic vocabulary is under-developed. (See Section 7.2.)

....

Summary

- The material in this section illustrates stronger and weaker student essays.
- The strengths and weaknesses relate to: writing skills (such as the use of paragraphs and transitions); the structure of the argument; content; and social scientific skills (such as the use of theory and evidence).
- Analysing the essays will help you identify what constitutes effective social scientific essay writing.

....

12   CONCLUDING REMARKS

....

Having submitted your essay, what next? First, enjoy briefly that 'It's done!' euphoria.

Then, if you haven't already done so, and before your marked essay comes back, read through the advice in Appendix A. Make a note of any key points of feedback, reflect on these and bear them in mind when working on your next assignment.

Writing academic essays in the social sciences is probably very different from any other writing you have done before, but it is central to getting your degree. It is hoped that by knowing what is required, and the techniques that help, you will not only feel more at ease writing your essays but will be able to demonstrate your knowledge and understanding to maximum effect. We are optimistic that you will find this guide a valuable resource that will help you on your way to *good essay writing*!

APPENDIX A
WHAT TO DO WHEN YOUR ESSAY COMES BACK

Maggie Coats

....

[Maggie Coats is an Associate Lecturer in the OU and here are her suggestions for learning from your last essay.]

If you're like most other people, when you get an essay back you'll check the grade first, read any general comments from your tutor and quickly flip through the rest looking for any major embarrassments. You'll probably read it with more care only if the tutor has written something particularly compli-mentary or irritating. However, learning from previous pieces of writing is an important way of building on your writing skills.

- Take a quick look at the score and any general comments. Feel pleased, angry or despairing, depending on your grade/ mood, then put the essay aside until you are ready to look at it with a more 'objective' eye.
- Give yourself twenty to thirty minutes to look over the essay in detail.
- Re-read any general comments and note the main points.
- Re-read the essay itself, including any more specific com-ments made by your tutor; mark your responses to these comments. Do you agree or disagree? Is there anything you don't understand?
- Next, re-read your tutor's general comments. Can you see what the tutor is saying?
- Do you agree with the grade? If not, make a note of it and raise this with your tutor. Is there anything that you still don't understand? Make a note and ask your tutor.

- On a separate sheet, write down one or two key points that will improve your performance when writing the next assignment. File these.

Source: adapted from Coats, undated, Handout Material 2.

APPENDIX B
PROCESS AND COMMAND WORDS
IN ESSAY QUESTIONS

Sue Cole and Pauline Harris

....

[Sue Cole, an OU Associate Lecturer, and Pauline Harris, an OU Assistant Staff Tutor, offer the following explanations for the command words that you're likely to find in essay questions.]

Account for	Explain, clarify, give reasons for.
Analyse	Resolve into its component parts. Examine critically or minutely.
Assess	Determine the value of, weigh up (see also Evaluate).
Compare	Look for similarities and differences between, perhaps reach conclusions about which is preferable and justify this clearly.
Contrast	Set in opposition in order to bring out the differences sharply.
Compare and contrast	Find some points of common ground between x and y and show where or how they differ.
Criticize	Make a judgement (backed by a discussion of the evidence or reasoning involved) about the merit of theories or opinions or about the truth of facts.
Define	State the exact meaning of a word or phrase. In some cases it may be necessary or desirable to examine

	different possible or often used definitions.
Describe	Give a detailed account of . . .
Discuss	Explain, then give two sides of the issue and any implications.
Distinguish or differentiate between	Look for differences between . . .
Evaluate	Make an appraisal of the worth/validity/effectiveness of something in the light of its truth or usefulness (see also Assess).
Examine the argument that . . .	Look in detail at this line of argument.
Explain	Give details about how and why it is . . .
How far . . .	To what extent . . . Usually involves looking at evidence/arguments for and against and weighing them up.
Illustrate	Make clear and explicit. Usually requires the use of carefully chosen examples.
Justify	Show adequate grounds for decisions or conclusions, answer the main objections likely to be made about them.
Outline	Give the main features or general principles of a subject, omitting minor details and emphasizing structure and arrangement.
State	Present in a brief, clear way.
Summarize	Give a concise, clear explanation or account of . . . presenting the chief factors and omitting minor details and examples (see also Outline).
What arguments can be made for and against the view that . . .	Look at both sides of this argument.

Source: adapted from Cole and Harris, undated, Handout Material 2.

APPENDIX C
WORDSTORMING: EXAMPLES OF 'MIND MAPS'

....

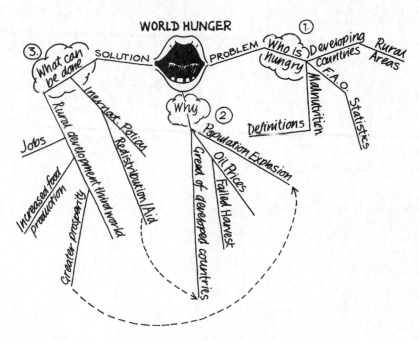

Figure C.1   *A mind map relating to an essay question on the causes of world malnutrition and its possible solutions*
Source: P.N.L. Study Guides, 1992

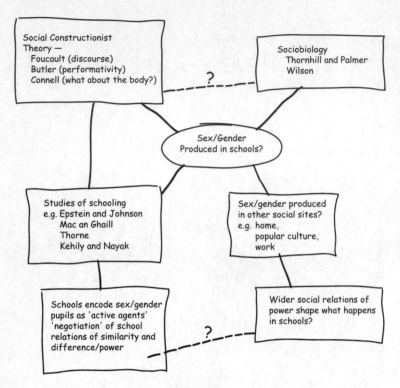

Figure C.2   *A more focused mind map relating to the Section 11 essay question on the production of sex/gender in schools*

APPENDIX D
MORE ON REFERENCING

....

Section 9 gives guidance and examples for the following printed sources:

- printed books (single and more than one author),
- edited collections,
- journal/periodical articles,
- newspaper article.

This appendix illustrates the following:

- electronic sources,
- personal communication,
- identifying the details for references,
- OU courses/course material.

Printed sources

- **An author quoted in another text**
  Sometimes you will come across a quotation or reference in a book you are reading and decide to reference it in your own work. In such circumstances it is good practice to go back to the original source to check that the details are correct (for example, has the original author been misquoted or her argument distorted?). However, particularly if the source is obscure or long out of print, this may not be possible. Furthermore, you may need to acknowledge that it was not you who identified this source but the author of the work you were reading. In such cases, the abbreviated reference would look like this, '(Drake, quoted in Weedon, 1999, p.7)', while the full reference would read:

  Weedon, C. (1999) *Feminism, Theory and the Politics of Difference*, Oxford, Blackwell.

(OU students should note the guidance given in the box at the end of this appendix.)

- **Government/official publication**
  For this source type the abbreviated reference would be '(Department of Social Security, 1999)' and the full details in the list of references:
  Department of Social Security (1999) 'Action across the UK', *Opportunity for All: Tackling Poverty and Social Exclusion*, London, The Stationery Office (September, Cm 4445).

- **Non-governmental organization publication**
  For this source type the abbreviated reference would be '(British Psychological Society, 1997)' and the full details in the list of references:
  British Psychological Society (1997) *Code of Conduct, Ethical Principles and Guidelines*, Leicester, British Psychological Society.

Electronic sources

Follow the conventions given above for printed material as best you can (including the conventions for the abbreviated reference in the essay text), although you will be aware that online sources are presented in considerably more forms than we have been used to with conventional print sources and it's only possible here to include a few of the many types you will encounter. Look out for the usual details and for online sources also include the name of the site and 'location' details (the URL) and the date you visited the site, as in, for example:

http://www.worldbank.org/devforum/about.html (accessed 27 July 2000).

The URL must be absolutely correct and given in full. The copyright line giving publication details is often placed at the foot of the first screen, so you may need to scroll down to find it. If the source is not online, include the medium (e.g. CD-ROM).
Some examples of the full reference details are given below.

- **Book**
Books that are freely available as complete texts online are often out of copyright and so do not usually carry publication details. Otherwise, you may, for example, want to reference a book you have bought as an e-book or accessed by joining a net library, and these will have place of publication and publisher details.

  For example:
  Mill, J.S. (1859) *On Liberty*, http://www.bartleby.com/130/index.html (accessed 28 January 2000).

  and:
  Shields, G. and Walton, G. (1998) *Cite them right!* Newcastle, University of Northumbria, http://www.unn.ac.uk/central/isd/cite/index.htm (accessed 9 February 2000).

- **Journal/periodical article**
Sommers, R.C. (1997) 'The quilting bee: a research metaphor', *The Qualitative Report*, vol.3, no.4, http://www.nova.edu/sss/QR3-4/sommers.html (accessed 9 February 1999).

- **Newspaper article**
Kettle, M. (2000) 'Hague tries to take a leaf from Republicans' Bush', *The Guardian*, 1 August, http://www.guardianunlimited.co.uk/politics/story/0,3604,349143,00.html (accessed 1 August 2000).

- **Government/official publication**
Home Office (2000) 'Introduction', *Government Policy Around Domestic Violence*, Home Office, http://www.home-office.gov.uk/epd/cpsu/domviol98.htm (accessed 16 June 2000, last updated 2 March 2000)

- **Non-governmental organization publication**
Amnesty International (2000) 'Russian federation. Raid on the Glasnost foundation by Special Police', *Amnesty International report EUR 46/40/00*, 31 August, http://www.amnesty.org/ailib/aipub/2000/EUR/44604000.htm (accessed 11 September 2000).

- **Research project**
Banks, N. (1996) 'Cultural values and the adoption of energy efficient technologies', *Postgraduate Research Projects*

> *Annual Report*, ECU, http://www.ecu.ox.ac.uk/annrep96/
> postgrad.htm (accessed 27 July 2000).

- **Conference**
  Kelly, B. (9 June 2000, 10:54) *ESSIR 2000 – European Summer School in Information Retrieval*, lis-elib@ mailbase.ac.uk (accessed 27 July 2000).

- **CD-ROM**
  Craig, E. (ed.) (1998) *Encyclopedia of Philosophy* [CD-ROM], London, Routledge.

Personal communication

If you quote something said in a conversation or letter, you should note this: '(Mac an Ghaill, 2000, personal conversation with author)'. You may not need to include this in the references list, but if you need to (e.g. if you have quoted directly or used any substantial points from your source) then you should add the initials to the list of references.

Identifying the details for references

Publication details are given near the front of the book on the 'imprint' page, which usually comes after the title page. Please check carefully the particular notes for each component (date, edition, place, publisher).

Different publication dates

The date of publication you need is the latest year noted in the book that you have. For instance, *The German Ideology*, a key text in classical Marxist theory, first appeared in the nineteenth century. However, our copy was published in 1974. This reference will read:

> Marx, K. and Engels, F. (1974) *The German Ideology*, London, Lawrence and Wishart.

Where dates for reprints are noted, use the year given against the copyright (©) line.

Retaining early publication dates

For quoted material from an early work, where you want to include the early date but your quotation is from a modern reproduction, note the later date first, separated from the original date by a slash. For example, for *The German Ideology*, the abbreviated reference would be: '(Marx, 1974/1846)'. The full reference would also include the date: '(1974/1846)'.

Edition numbers

Books are not only reprinted but they can be revised and republished as a new *edition*. This often occurs when new material is added because the book has become dated. In fact, our 1974 copy of *The German Ideology* is the second edition of this particular version of the book. A first edition was published in 1970. Because second and subsequent editions contain alterations, it is important to tell the reader which version you're working from. This reference should therefore read:

> Marx, K. and Engels, F. (1974/1846) *The German Ideology*, 2nd edn, London, Lawrence and Wishart.

Publisher and place of publication

Assuming that you are writing in Britain or for a British audience, you need to quote the British place of publication of British publishers. For example, Sage is based in London, so you put London as the place of publication; Open University Press (a company separate from The Open University itself) is based in Buckingham, so you put Buckingham. However, some books that you reference may be published overseas and imported into Britain. In such cases you need to indicate that the book is an overseas publication.

Be sure to give the place of publication (that is, the city or town where the publisher is based) and not the place where the book was printed.

Collaborative publishing

Sometimes books are brought out by more than one publisher. OU course books are often collaborations of this kind. In such cases, name both publishers. The place of publication will be indicated on the imprint page. An abbreviated reference could be '(Evans and Hall, 1999)'. It would carry the full reference:

> Evans, J. and Hall, S. (1999) *Visual Culture: The Reader*, London, Sage/The Open University.

Advice for OU students

These are the conventions for OU students when referencing OU course material or authors quoted/referred to in OU course material.

OU courses/course material

In the social sciences, most written OU course material is identifiable by the author's name and can be referenced as such. For example, a chapter written by OU academic Gail Lewis for the course D218 *Social Policy: Welfare, Power and Diversity* would be referenced as '(Lewis, 1998)' in the text of the essay and as follows in your list of references at the end of the essay:

> Lewis, G. (1998) 'Welfare and the social construction of "race"', in Saraga, E. (ed.) *Embodying the Social: Constructions of Difference*, London, Routledge/The Open University.

However, some course materials are not co-published. In these cases, the publisher should be identified as the University itself; for example:

Mooney, G., Kelly, B., Goldblatt, D. and Hughes, G. (2000) DD100 *Introductory Chapter. Tales of Fear and Fascination: The Crime Problem in the Contemporary UK*, Milton Keynes, The Open University.

An author quoted/referred to in OU course material

Some of what you quote from or refer to will be material that is cited in the OU course you are studying. For example, you may want to use the following quotation by Edmund Leach:

> The prototype of the stage Irishmen . . . is not so much a figure of fun as an object of contempt merging into deep hostility. . . . The ethnic element in 'Irish' jokes is . . . blatantly racist. (Leach, 1979, pp.viii–ix)

This quotation appears in a chapter called 'Welfare and the social construction of "race"' by Gail Lewis in the OU course, D218 *Social Policy: Welfare, Power and Diversity*. How should it be referenced?

As we suggested above (in respect of an author quoted in another text), strictly speaking, you should go back to the original source, check the accuracy of the citation, then reference this original text. This is neither practical nor required of you as an OU student. In the context of your OU writing, we suggest that you simply provide the reference as given in your OU course material. Thus, in the above case the abbreviated reference after the quotation would read, '(Leach, 1979, pp.viii–ix, quoted in Lewis, 1998, p. 134)', and the full reference would read:

> Leach, E. (1979) 'The official Irish jokesters', *New Society*, 20–27 December, pp.vii–ix, cited in Lewis, G. (1998) 'Welfare and the social construction of "race"' in Saraga, E. (ed.) *Embodying the Social: Constructions of Difference*, London, Routledge/The Open University.

Although this convention is technically correct, it is cumbersome and your tutor may be happy for you to reference only the original text, that is, '(Leach, 1979, pp. viii–ix)' and in full:

> Leach, E. (1979) 'The official Irish jokesters', *New Society*, 20–27 December, pp.vii–ix.

OU cassettes, television, radio programmes and other electronic media

Most material of this kind will not have an identifiable 'author'. In such circumstances, the 'author' should be identified as the University itself. For example, for an OU TV programme you would have in the text: '(The Open University, 1999)'. The full reference would need to include details as in the following examples:

> The Open University (1999) TV07 *The Agony and the Ecstasy: Moral Panics and Youth Culture*, DD100 *An Introduction to the Social Sciences: Understanding Social Change*, Milton Keynes, The Open University.

Here, the publication date refers to the date of recording, which should be given in the programme.

Similarly, the full reference for a cassette would give the publication date of the tape (printed on the cassette) and the other details similar to those for OU printed material:

> The Open University (1999) Audio-cassette 1, Side A *What are the Social Sciences?*, DD100 *An Introduction to the Social Sciences: Understanding Social Change*, Milton Keynes, The Open University.

APPENDIX E
ABBREVIATIONS AND WORDS IN
FOREIGN LANGUAGES

....

At various points in your reading, especially in references, you will come across various abbreviations or words written in foreign languages. You may need to use these in your own writing, so here's a list of some of the more common examples.

cf. (*confer*)	compare
ch., chs, (or chap., chaps)	chapter(s)
ed., eds	editor(s)
edn	edition
e.g. (*exempli gratia*)	'for example' (not to be confused with 'i.e.'). Used when an actual example is given, as in the following: 'Some forms of analysis (e.g. Marxist and feminist theories) suggest that social phenomena are the product of underlying and prior social divisions'.
et al. (*et alii*)	'and others', used for multiple authors as in '(Hatt et al., 1978)'
et seq. (et sequens)	'and the following' (for example, pp.16 et seq.)
ff.	alternative to *et seq.* (for example, pp.16 ff.)
ibid. (*ibidem*)	'in the same work' (as the last reference). Used in footnotes/ endnotes to save writing out the whole reference again (for example, 'Gilroy, ibid. p.61').
i.e. (*id est*)	'that is' (not to be confused with 'e.g.'). Used to explain, define or clarify as in the following: 'Radical feminists (i.e. feminists who

	maintain that gender relations are the product of a universal and unitary system of male dominance) argue that'.
loc. cit. (*loco citato*)	'in the same place' (as the previous passage)
n., nn.	note(s), as in 'p.4, n.2'
op. cit. (*opere citato*)	'in the work recently cited' as in 'Gilroy, op. cit., p.67'; used in footnotes/endnotes to save writing a full reference for a work previously cited, but not the last reference (cf. 'ibid.')
passim	throughout the work (not on one page only)
p., pp.	page, pages
q.v. (*quod vide*)	'which see' (for cross-referencing)
(*sic*)	'thus'; indicates that questionable/ apparently incorrect quoted material is faithfully reproduced from the original
trans., tr.	translator
vol., vols	volume(s)

APPENDIX F
FURTHER READING

....

There are many excellent books and resources that deal with writing skills. Those listed below are particularly relevant to essay writing skills at undergraduate level.

Cottrell, S. (2000) *The Study Skills Handbook*, London, Macmillan; ISBN: 0335751892.

Crème, P. and Lea, M.R. (1997) *Writing at University*, Buckingham, Open University Press; ISBN: 033519642X.

Hart, C. (1998) *Doing a Literature Review: Releasing the Social Science Research Imagination*, London, Sage/Open University; ISBN: 0761959750.

Johnson, R. (1996, 6th edn) *Writing Essays: Guidance Notes for Students*, Manchester, Clifton Press; ISBN: 0951984403.

Northedge, A. (1990) *The Good Study Guide*, Milton Keynes, The Open University; ISBN: 0749200448.

Oliver, P. (1996) *Teach Yourself – Writing Essays and Reports*, London, Hodder and Stoughton; ISBN: 034067010X.

Peck, J. and Coyle, M. (1999) *The Student's Guide to Writing: Grammar, Punctuation and Spelling*, London, Macmillan; ISBN: 0333727428.

Taylor, G. (1989) *The Student's Writing Guide for the Arts and Social Sciences*, Cambridge, Cambridge University Press; ISBN: 0521369053.

You may want to visit the Mantex home page at http://www.mantex.co.uk for further suggestions, resources, reviews and links (key in 'writing guides' in the search panel). For advice on the use of written English and academic writing skills, see also the Open University's 'Learner's Guide' website, 'Learning skills development' (go to http://www.open.ac.uk/learners-guide).

REFERENCES

BPS (1994) *Guidelines for External Examiners on Undergraduate Psychology Degrees*, Leicester, British Psychological Society/Association of Heads of Psychology Departments.

Coats, M. (undated) *Open Teaching Toolkit: Learning How to Learn*, Milton Keynes, The Open University.

Cole, S. and Harris, P. (undated) *Open Teaching Toolkit: Revision and Examinations*, Milton Keynes, The Open University.

Lewis, G. (1998) 'Welfare and the social construction of "race"', in Saraga, E. (ed.) *Embodying the Social: Constructions of Difference*, London, Routledge/The Open University.

Mac an Ghaill, M. (1999) *Contemporary Racisms and Ethnicities: Social and Cultural Transformations*, Buckingham, Open University Press.

P.N.L. Study Guides (1992) *How to Write Essays: Suggestions for Teaching Essay Writing*, London, Educational Development Service of the Polytechnic of North London.

Sherratt, N., Goldblatt, D., Mackintosh, M. and Woodward, K. (2000) DD100 *An Introduction to the Social Sciences: Understanding Social Change, Workbook 1*, Milton Keynes, The Open University.

The Open University (1994) 'Appendix B: some comments on essay writing', D309 *Cognitive Psychology, Assignments Booklet*, Milton Keynes, The Open University.

The Open University (1998) *Keyskills: Making a Difference*, Milton Keynes, The Open University/DfEE.

Rubin, D. (1983) *Teaching Reading and Study Skills in Content Areas*, London, Holt, Reinhart and Winston.

Weedon, C. (1999) *Feminism, Theory and the Politics of Difference*, Oxford, Blackwell.

ACKNOWLEDGEMENTS

....

Cartoons by Adrian Burrows; reproduced with permission from Robert Barrass (1982) *Students Must Write*, Andover, Routledge.

Appendix C Figure C.1 reproduced by permission of the University of North London.

INDEX